1/98

C

CRAZY
with
COTTON

Piecing Together
Memories & Themes

C&T PUBLISHING

Copyright©1996 Diana Leone
Developmental Editor: Liz Aneloski
Copy Editor: Judith M. Moretz
Technical Editor: Sally Lanzarotti
Illustrator: John Cram
Cover Design: John Cram and Kathy Lee
Cover Quilt: Diana Leone
Book Design: John Cram
Design Assistant: Micaela M. Carr
Cover Photography: Carina Woolrich
Photo Credits:

Diana Leone:
Pages 4–7, 10–12, 17 bottom, 18 top, 20 top, 21 bottom, 24 top, 25 top, 26–30, 32 bottom left, 32 top right, 33 center left, 33 bottom left, 33 top right, 33 center right, 35 bottom, 36 bottom, 37 bottom left, 37 center right, 39 bottom, 40 top left, 40 center left, 40, center right, 40 bottom right, 41 top right, 41 bottom left, 45, 47, 49, 50–67, 69–74, 75 top, 77 left, 82, 83, 88, 89, 96

Sharon Risedorph:
Pages 8, 13–17 top, 19, 23, 31, 32 top left, 32 center left , 37 top right, 44, 46, 48, 68, 77 right, 78–81, 84, 85

Jonathan Clark:
Pages 9, 18 bottom, 20 bottom, 21 top, 22, 24 center and bottom, 33 top left, 33 bottom right, 35 top, 36 top, 38, 39 top, 40 top right, 41 center right, 42, 75 bottom, 76, 86, 87, 90, 91

Diane Regan: Ed Leone:
Page 25 bottom   Author photo on back cover

Bernina is a registered trademark of Bernina of America.
Creative Grid© Diana Leone, manufactured by E. E. Schenck.
Disney characters © Disney Enterprises, Inc./
    Used by permission from Disney Enterprises, Inc.
Dual Shader is a trademark of Fabric Mate.
Euro Pro is a trademark of Euro Pro, Inc.
Fiskars is a registered trademark of Fiskars, Inc.
HeatnBond is a registered trademark of Therm O Web, Inc.
Metafil is a brand name of Sullivans.
Mettler Cordonnet and Metallic are brand names of Arova
    Mettler AG.
Needle Release is a trademark of Stan Rising.
Olfa is a registered trademark of Olfa Products Corporation.
Omnigrid is a registered trademark of Omnigrid Inc.
Patchwork Appliqué is a trademark of Diana Leone.
Photo Effects is a trademark of Hues, Inc.
Pigma Micron is a registered trademark of the Sakura Color
    Products Corporation of America.
Pimatex is a trademark of Robert Kaufman Co., Inc.
Plexiglas is a registered trademark of Rohn & Haas Company.
Rowenta is a registered trademark of Rowenta, Inc.
Sakura is a registered trademark of Sakura of America.
Schmetz is a brand name of Ferd. Schmetz GmbH., Germany
Sew Steady Portable Table is a product of Dream World
    Enterprises Inc.
Sharpie is a registered trademark of Sanford Corporation.
Sulky is a registered trademark of Sulky of America.
The Lion King is a registered trademark of the Walt Disney
    Company.
Versatex is a brand name of Siphon Art.
Viking is a registered trademark of VWS.
VIP is a registered trademark of VIP Corporation.
YLI is a registered trademark of YLI Corporation.

Dedication

TO THE QUILT

It is the quilt that brings us together, teaches us humility, encourages us to learn, and takes gratification in seeing us fly.

Acknowledgments

A special thank you to all the fabric designers and manufacturers who have so generously shared their extensive knowledge, future fabric designs, and the latest fabric samples for my study and use.

Another big thank you to all the quilt dealers who, over the past twenty years, have gotten to know my tastes and have brought me the very best quilts for my study and collection.

A third thank you to all the quilters who have made this book possible.

And last, but certainly not least, to Joan Chamberlain and the many friends, contributors, and entire staff at C&T (especially Kathy, Liz, Sally, Diane, and John) who continue so generously and professionally to give their patience, guidance, and expertise to make this book possible.

ISBN #1-57120-017-7

Library of Congress Cataloging-in-Publication
Leone, Diana
    Crazy with cotton : piecing together memories and themes / Diana Leone.
        p.   cm.
    Includes bibliographical references.
    ISBN 1-57120-017-7 (pbk.)
    1. Patchwork. 2. Crazy quilts. 3. Cotton fabrics. I. Title.
TT835.L45497 1996
746.46--dc20   96-32733

Printed in Hong Kong
10 9 8 7 6 5 4 3 2 1

Contents

Crazy Quilt Card, Eddie Leone, Jr.

Introduction

Quilts are the fabric of my life. I have spent the past twenty-five years teaching and encouraging people to make quilts an integral part of their own history. I want to make quilting so compelling that, once interested, it will be impossible for my students, customers, and friends not to continue to include some aspect of quilting in their lives. It doesn't matter how they choose to incorporate quilting; whether they read about it, study one aspect of the craft, fuse, hand or machine sew, appliqué, or patch. The most important thing is the appreciation of the quilt, and the passing on of a time-honored tradition.

My shop, like my life, revolves around quilting. The Quilting Bee is a safe haven, a gathering place for both the novice and experienced quilter, and for meeting with friends, old and new. Conversations about fabrics and quilting techniques with customers and students became the inspiration for many of my books, this one included.

My collection of fabric can only be described as massive. This fabric collection is both a library and a palette ready for my artistic use. I no longer feel the need to justify any fabric purchase. As a quiltmaker and artist I cannot worry about leftovers, scraps, or unused yards of fabric.

If I were a chef, I would have the most up-to-date equipment, gleaming copper pots, the latest cookbooks, and—most important—the choicest ingredients. The same applies to quilting. Having the right equipment makes the process more successful and enjoyable. (See Tools and Supplies chapter beginning on page 19.)

Quilting becomes easier and more productive if you work to acquire and maintain a full collection of a wide variety of fabrics. Stopping to find a perfect fabric could delay the creative process by stifling the moment's inspiration, but we continue to make the trip to the quilt shop in search of that one fabric we need to finish the design. To create a masterpiece quilt, I think of fabric as the palette and the sewing machine as a brush. The canvas is the challenge to have fun, make quilts, and share them with you.

The antique quilt shown on page 9 was the inspiration for this book. Notice how it is made up of strip pieced blocks that portray a theme. The blocks consist of a multiple-sided center fabric with fabric strips sewn around the center. This block is the basis from which all of the quilts in this book were created. These quilts were developed around themes and memories.

It is our memories, like the pieces of a quilt, that remind us of who we are, where we came from, and where we would like to be. So this book is written for you, the textile collector, the fabric artist, the quilter, and the person wishing to begin a new and enjoyable project that may become an important piece of your personal history.

Block detail of *Grover Cleveland Cretonne Quilt*. See quilt on page 9.

Early History Of Crazy Quilts

THE VICTORIAN CRAZY QUILT

Victorian crazy quilts we are most familiar with were made during the Victorian era, spanning the years 1878 to 1900. These quilts were made of bits and pieces of printed fabrics, velvets, and silks, and enhanced with elaborate embroidery stitches and other needlework embellishments.

Victorian Crazy Quilt. Scraps of velvets and silks sewn to a foundation cloth. Quilt includes fabric painting, tobacco silk ribbon, and embroidery of typical flora and fauna of the day.

Detail of Abraham Lincoln, U.S. President from 1861-1865. Presidential ribbon was sewn into this Victorian crazy quilt. Collection of Diana Leone.

Fabric painted floral motif on silk

5

Historically, part of a young gentlewoman's education during this time (intended as training for her ultimate role as wife of the household) included hours of sewing. The techniques for making fine pieces of crewel work and needlepoint were joined by patchwork and appliqué that had become very popular in America. But society dictated that these women of the upper class should not make patchwork and appliqué quilts similar to those of the more common folk. So, to set themselves apart, the fancy silk and velvet crazy quilts were created to satisfy the desire to quilt, and yet still display the fine stitchery that was the mark of a refined Victorian lady.

In a time when "more was better," the challenge was to create as large a variety of stitches and decoration as one could put into one quilt top. These women had access to the beautiful silk and velvet scraps left by their dressmakers. By combining opulent fabrics and decorative stitches, they developed the basic designs for the Victorian crazy quilts we know and love today. Ultimately, this art form was to last until the beginning of the twentieth century, but the women who created these quilts left a legacy of an elite handcraft that remains inspirational to this day.

DOLL QUILT CIRCA 1840, 24″ x 24″,
Collection of Diana Leone.

Very early doll quilt. A rare example of a cotton crazy quilt, probably from England.

THE COTTON CRAZY QUILT

From the cave paintings of our ancestors to modern-day art collections, it is obvious that we have always found the need to decorate our surroundings. In the development of art throughout history, people who could not afford to purchase art, found ways to copy and create their own "folk art." The cotton crazy quilt is one of the best examples of a folk art that owes its creation to a more "refined" beginning.

Although we can date the Victorian crazy quilt era, it is difficult to say just when the first cotton crazy quilt was designed and sewn. Its beginning came from frugality, the need to create warmth, and the desire to emulate the beauty of Victorian crazy quilts.

To recreate Victorian crazy quilts, quiltmakers used a variety of inexpensive printed, pictorial fabrics that copied the more expensive decorator chintzes of the day. Printed fabrics were used in place of the silk ribbons, oil paintings, fancy beading, and laces found in more traditional Victorian crazy quilts. These fabric imitations were the storytellers of the era, and were readily available and inexpensive, making it possible for most people to decorate in the most stylish modes of the time.

Block detail of *Grover Cleveland Cretonne Quilt*. See quilt on page 9. Zebra family printed on decorator cotton fabric.

In the past, just as today, people read books and newspapers, saw what beauty others had created, and copied or modified various designs to fit their own tastes and pocketbooks. For an experienced quilter, all that was needed was to sketch a rough diagram, find some scraps, develop a personalized design, and start cutting and stitching. Thus, folk art became a chronicle of daily life.

The cotton crazy quilt you make will become a personal documentation of your story, or theme, told through the contemporary "conversational" fabrics you will select.

It is important to write your story, include it on the back of your quilt, and sign your name.

Block detail of *Grover Cleveland Cretonne Quilt*. See quilt on page 9. Child's nursery story illustration printed on "cretonne," a conversational fabric from 1880.

Cotton Crazy Quilt, circa 1890, 68" x 56", 6" block
Collection of Diana Leone.

Cotton crazy quilt made from the scraps of fabric given to an African American slave. This quilt shows the need to create a work of art as interpreted by the maker. Bits and pieces of fabric were sewn to a foundation cloth. Crazy pieced blocks create the center. String pieced Log Cabin blocks were added to three sides. Did she run out of blocks, or was she being creative? This 1890 mint-condition quilt is a masterpiece of design and use of fabrics.

GROVER CLEVELAND CRETONNE QUILT, 1884, 72" x 72", 12" block
Collection of Diana Leone.

This cretonne quilt top was the inspiration for this book. After I purchased this quilt in 1987 I hung it above the desk in my office. It is one of my most treasured quilts. People would make a point to look at it when they visited, often asking about its history. In 1988 I sent the quilt to Pat Nichols, who had offered to research the top and document it for me. Pat provided some interesting information that inspired me to investigate this intriguing quilt further. As time passed and I began to learn more about the storytelling fabrics of today, and of times past, I grew to appreciate this unique quilt more and more. I look at the quilt and wish I could hear all the stories the quiltmaker could tell.

The Evolution of Storytelling Fabrics

I find it fascinating that the prints of yesterday remain so popular today, and I am very glad we have nostalgic, historic "retro" prints available for our use. Retro prints are fabrics that reflect a theme or style from the past.

The fabrics you will choose to piece into your quilt will tell a story, record events and passing fads, as well as date the quilt. I have collected fabrics for over thirty years. My extensive quilt collection includes at least one sampler quilt from each ten-year period from 1840 to 1990. These quilts are a catalogue of the prints made during each specific time frame. In researching how these fabrics were made, I learned not only about the textile industry, but all sorts of interesting social history as well. The fabrics in this book represent just a very few of the thousands of prints that have been available. These early printed fabrics led to the conversationals or theme prints we see in such great abundance today. Conversationals are some of the fabrics you can use in your cotton crazy quilts.

1880s Cretonne

1930s Bark cloth

1994 Holiday

1990s

1930s Chicago World's Fair

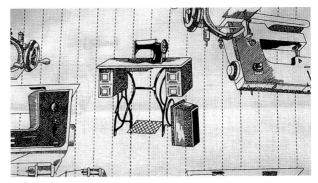

1990s Toile

1930s Hawaiian sugar sack

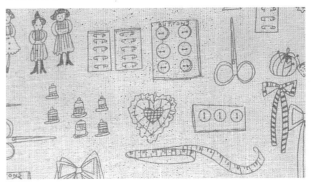

1990s Toile

1990s Retro print (1950s)

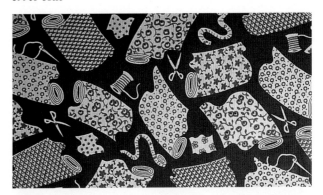

1940s

1960s Hawaiian

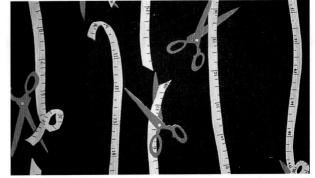

1950s

CHEATER CLOTH

I am fascinated by the continued printing of printed patchwork, "cheater cloth," as it is called. I have found it, from the 1870s to the present. The Grover Cleveland quilt on page 9 includes two examples of printed patchwork which documents the fact that different patchwork prints have continued to be made over a long period of time. If the folk artist didn't have the time or inclination to piece fabric, the patchwork fabric could be used. The fact that the textile printer would print such a design is even more amazing. They had to realize the importance of the patchwork quilt and the need for such a "fool the eye" fabric in both home decorating and sewing.

TOILES DU JOUY

Toiles du Jouy are floral or scenic designs first printed in France in 1786 by Christopher Philip Oberkampf. These story fabrics became the most sought after fabrics for home decorating. The inexpensive "cretonne" conversationals of 1880 and 1940 were a result of the early picture fabrics. The line drawings depict the flora and fauna of the past and present. Toiles are still printed today and are as popular in home decorating now as when they were originally created. As an alternative to actual toiles, look for panel prints that have instructions printed on the fabrics. The instructions contain small black and white pictures that can be used as today's toiles.

1884, "chinoisere" printed on nine-patch cheater cloth

1850, toile, England or France

1880, sailing ship, bird, crazy quilt stitches on cretonne cheater cloth

1786, toile, rare detail from Oberkampf. This fine example illustrates the quality of line drawn etching printed on cloth.

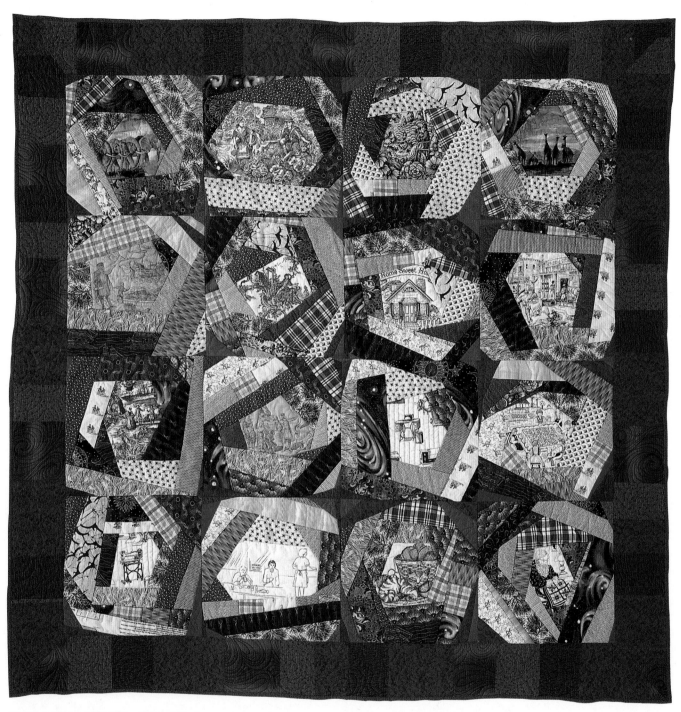

TOILES DU JOUY, 1994, 72" x 72", 14" block
Diana Leone
machine pieced , machine quilted

One color prints, or toiles, were used in Diana's quilter's memory
quilt. The toiles were selected from very fine decorator fabrics and
small vignettes found in panel prints. Monochromatic prints were
used in the strips to add color and cohesiveness. The bicycle print is
from a line of fabrics printed in 1990, designed by Diana Leone.

PRINTS THROUGH TIME

Printed fabrics have always been helpful to the quilt historian, thanks to the thorough documentation of the textile printing industry. Today's quilts can sometimes be dated to a particular month and year. Some of today's historic clues can be found in juvenile prints. In 1885 a Kate Greenaway figure would be rolling a hoop with a stick, whereas today's youngsters would be shown wearing in-line skates. In a 1910 copper roller print you would find a line drawing of a child riding a tricycle. In 1950 a fabric motif might include children playing with hula hoops. Today's juvenile fabrics would include children playing with electronic toys.

1940s

1980s

1990s

1950s

1920s

Enjoy the Prints of Today

We are in one of the longest and largest print cycles in the history of the textile industry. We are all the recipients of this bounty of prints. It is very exciting to be a part of the quilt industry today, with many fabrics being printed specifically for the quilt-maker. As people buy more ready-made items for their homes and wardrobes, the quilt industry is keeping the over-the-counter textile industry alive.

Future historians will delight in seeing the prints of the 1990s. Use any of your collection of prints or mix them with current prints. Never before could you find leaping frogs in five colors, baseball, football, Betty Boop, and Elvis theme prints. You will find fabrics with sewing implements, musical instruments, carpentry tools, and even quilters quilting away. Imagine having over twenty-seven different cat and kitten fabrics at one time from which to choose, in just one season. You'll find fabrics with cars, horses, toys, food, fruit, mountains, clouds, bricks, trees, ducks, geese, chickens, and people from around the world.

In the new "City Lights" fabrics you can see scenes of San Francisco that include Japantown, the Bay Bridge, and cable cars.

I hope you will use *Crazy with Cotton* as an excuse to document and pictorialize your lives, hobbies, or important occasions.

Possibilities

African Pillows, Luanne Cohen

Shamrock Pillow, Kathy Galos

Kitten Pillows,
Diana Leone

Crazy Quilt Card and Here's My Heart
Mini-quilt, Diana Leone

Crazy Quilt Cards, Mary Jo Vogelsang

Crazy Quilt Card, Mary Jo Vogelsang

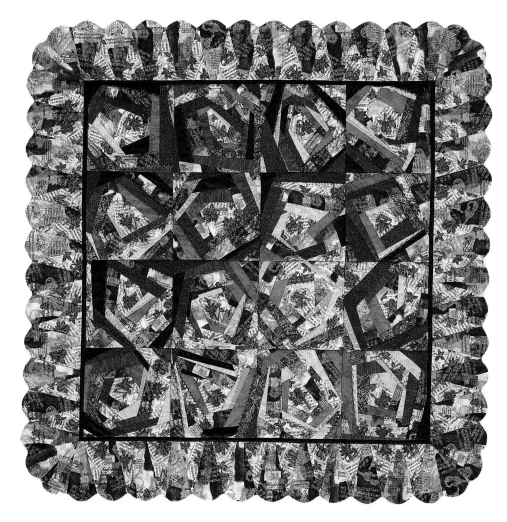

HOME FOR THE HOLIDAYS, 1995, 56" x 56", 14" block
Mary Jo Vogelsang
machine pieced, machine quilted

Mary Jo chose fabrics that coordinate with her Christmas decor. The theme fabric includes musical instruments and poinsettias. This crazy quilt is a more contemporary rendition of the traditional block featured in this book.

Patchwork Jacket,
Diana Leone

Patchwork Sweatshirt,
Diana Leone

MUFASA AND GANG IN KITAMBAALAND, 1995, 43" x 47"
Virginia Schnalle
various block sizes, machine pieced, machine quilted

The inspiration for this quilt was twofold. Virginia's grandson loved Disney's *The Lion King*, and a local quilt shop issued a challenge using P&B Textiles's African-style Kitambaa fabrics and Kaufman's Pointillist fabrics. Virginia varied the block sizes and utilized the prints to their best advantage, trying to achieve the whimsical lion look. This wonderful quilt received the P&B "Best Use of Fabrics" award.

HUMPHREY AND FRIENDS, 1995, 60" x 66", 12" block
Kelly Simbirdi
machine pieced, machine quilted

The whale fabric is showcased in the traditional Attic Window pattern, inspired by the book *Attic Windows— A Contemporary View* by Diana Leone, 1980. The use of the primary colors and the Attic Window pattern add the three dimensional depth. It looks like you are in a submarine looking out the windows.

AFRICAN DREAMS, 1995, 72" x 86", 13$^1/_2$" block
Luanne Seymour Cohen
machine pieced, machine quilted

African theme fabrics were used to coordinate and decorate
the Cohen's living room. Mettler Cordonnet topstitching
thread was used to machine appliqué the fabric motifs to the
top. The quilting designs were traced from the fabric designs,
then machine quilted in the border using topstitching thread.

SPORTS AND GOOD FOOD, 1994, 46" x 58", 12" block
Charlie Enscore
machine pieced, hand appliquéd

Charlie used the theme prints of hockey and junk food to make this quilt for her nephew. The use of the texture fabrics around the centers helps to frame the centers and adds a masculine touch. The fabrics used in the centers were brought over the seam's edge and appliquéd to the block after the block was completed. This technique of Patchwork Appliqué™ was developed by Diana Leone in 1987.

TRADITIONAL AMISH GONE A LITTLE CRAZY, 1994, 32" x 32", 9" block
Kathleen Azevedo
machine pieced, hand quilted

This quilt is an excellent example of how a traditional quilt style can be adapted to a crazy quilt. The large center areas were used to showcase nine different hand quilted patterns. The quilting designs were adapted to fit into the shapes of the blocks' centers, so the quilt is just a little bit crazy. Solid fabrics, in the shades of the colors, give this quilt the rich appearance of the Amish style.

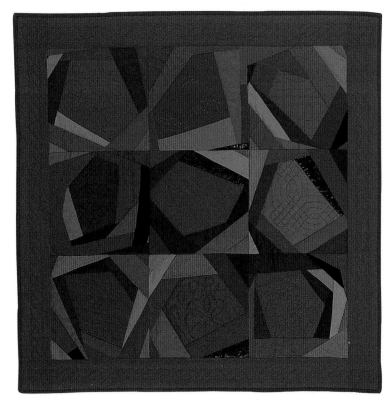

HOT CHILI SALSA, 1994, 54" x 86", 16" block
Charlie Enscore
machine pieced, machine quilted

One "hot" fabric was showcased in each center. The south of the border theme was reinforced in the selection of the tropical fabrics that were used for the strips. The border was made of large crazy patch blocks cut from point to point.

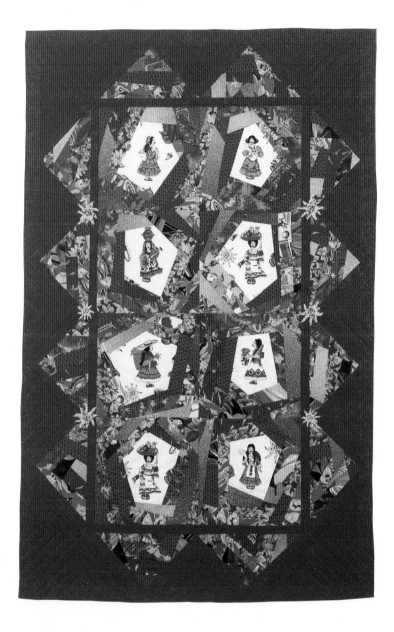

CACTUS CRAZED, 1993, 18" x 12^1/$_4$", 6" block
Cheryl Greider Bradkin
machine pieced, machine quilted

Cheryl has been sewing Seminole patchwork quilts since 1977 and is the author of *Basic Seminole Patchwork*. This piece was sewn as a sample for a workshop she developed on using Seminole patchwork in Crazy Log Cabin blocks. Each block is worked on a foundation cut to the finished block size. The shape of each center—cut from a theme print—determines the number of sides (or "logs") that surround the center. Using Seminole patchwork bands for some of the logs adds a certain vitality to the blocks; and using the same fabric as the last log on each block creates the effect of sashing and unites the piece.

COWBOY QUILT, 1995, 60" x 84", 12" block
Kathy Galos
machine pieced, machine quilted.

Kathy used the resurgence of the western prints as a resource to collect everything she could find to follow her theme. Notice the block set in this quilt. The blocks are moved over each other in alternating rows. The half blocks were made to use the long narrow cowboy prints. If you make full blocks to fill in the rows, remember to add the extra vertical seam allowances to allow for the cutting and piecing of the half blocks.

OTOMODACHI, 1993, 52" x 67", 12" block
Charlene Hughes
machine pieced, machine quilted

This quilt is named *Otomodachi* ("Friends") because most of the wonderful stash Charlene used was donated by special people in her life. The rectangle blocks are made on a foundation fabric. A Japanese palette of black and white with accents of red was used. Charlene used a small amount of sashiko quilting for an accent. The border is made of a salvaged yukata cloth. Although Charlene has often worked with silks and old kimono fabric, this was her first use of Japanese cottons in a quilt. The asymmetrical effect is a traditional Japanese theme.

GWENDOLYN'S CATS AND KITTENS, 1996, 22" x 36", 7" block
Diana Leone
machine pieced, tied with yarn

Children love small quilts. This quilt was made for Diana's seven-year-old granddaughter to play with, use, and enjoy. To involve her in the making of the quilt, Gwendolyn selected the fabrics and arranged the blocks. This quilt is a wonderful way to use leftover scraps and all the cat fabric you've collected. The backing is pieced using a rectangle of a large cat print pieced to blue flannel borders. The flannel edges were brought to the front and machine hemmed. The quilt has a fluffy batting and was hand tied with yarn since Gwendolyn likes "those soft things on the front."

VINTAGE BLOCKS AND FLOUR SACKS, 40" x 40", 12" block
Kathy Galos
machine pieced, machine tacked

Kathy featured some of her 1930s vintage blocks in this quilt. Scraps from other 1930s quilt projects were used to complete the quilt. The vintage blocks were set on point on foundation blocks and then strips were added. This is a great idea for old blocks, new pieced blocks, friendship blocks, kid's blocks, etc. The quilt top and backing were sewn right sides together, then turned right side out and tacked. No binding or batting.

Block from original 1930s string pineapple quilt that inspired Kathy Galos's 1930s reproduction. Collection of Diana Leone.

'30S STRING PINEAPPLE, 1995, 32" by 32", 16" block
Kathy Galos
machine pieced

This quilt was inspired by a vintage String Pineapple quilt. Kathy used the cotton crazy technique to create blocks with a small center surrounded by a variety of narrow fabric strips. The many-sided small centers and the use of narrow strips resulted in a scrap pineapple design. Although the centers are old feed sacks, the remaining fabrics are reproductions. The quilt top and backing were sewn with right sides together, then turned right side out. No batting or binding.

Fun for Kids (or any beginner)

Pillow

The cotton crazy piecing technique is easy and fun for the young person and new sewer.

The child can help select the fabric, decide on a "theme," and use this project to practice sewing.

Complete instructions begin on page 49.

MATERIALS:
Crazy patch block trimmed to 15" square,
15" x 15" square for pillow backing
Loose fill or 14" x 14" pillow form

1 Make a 16" x 16" (unfinished) crazy patch block following instructions beginning on page 49.
2 Trim the crazy patch block to 15" x 15" as shown on page 59.
3 Pin the crazy patch block and the pillow backing with right sides together.
4 Sew a 1/2" seam around all four sides, leaving a 4" opening.
5 Turn the pillow right side out.
6 Fill the pillow with loose fill.
7 Pin the edges of the opening together.
8 Sew the opening closed by hand.
9 Sign your name on the back.

Tips for Working with Kids

- One block made into a pillow is a good first project.
- Let the child select the fabric for the center.
- An adult can precut some centers and strips.
- Cut centers with a point at the top, not a flat edge.
- The strips should be 14" or longer.
- The strips can extend 2" beyond the edge of the foundation square.
- Use any part of the strip.
- Do not cut the strips even with the foundation fabric edge until sewing is done.
- It's o.k. to make scraps out of the leftovers.
- Beginners think they should cut small pieces to fill in around the edges. Use long strips when sewing the last areas near the edges.
- The foundation may become crooked as the block is being sewn.

Left to right: Elise, Patrick, Heather, Diana, Kathy, and Max

KRAZY FOR KATS
Heather Regan
four 10" x 10" blocks
2" sashing, 2" border
right sides sewn together,
turned right side out,
machine tacked,
thin batt

Heather loves to sew. She selected all the fabrics for each block from an assortment of pre-cut centers and strips. The theme is cats and kittens. Heather wanted to use as many different prints as she could find.

Patrick's quilt and yardage requirements are featured on page 82 and 83.

Patrick Galos at the sewing machine

Elise Ryan, age 9, proudly displaying her crazy quilt

Starburst
Elise Ryan
four 12" x 12" blocks
6" border
sun cut free form,
topstitched by machine,
"raw edge applique,"
machine quilted by
Elise, thin batt

Tools & Supplies

The supplies and materials listed are recommended as some of the best products available at the time of this printing. Our industry is always coming up with new products, and some supplies are more readily available than others. The supplies are listed with brand names in case you need to purchase any of them. I have tested these items and recommend them for their quality, versatility, and ease of use. They are not, however, the only products that will work. If you have something similar and it works for you, please use it. Refer to the Buyer's Guide on page 96 to order any of the products listed, or ask your favorite quilt shop to order for you.

Sewing Machine

Buy the best machine you can afford, and always keep it in good working order. Make sure your machine is well-tuned, oiled, and cleaned. I clean mine almost every time I use it. Vacuum the lint from under the feed dogs, oil if needed, and check the tension guides for loose threads and lint. Use a new needle every six to eight hours of sewing, and sew with the best cotton thread you can find.

Extension Table

The Sew Steady Portable Table will extend your working surface up to twenty inches and may be purchased to fit any model of sewing machine. This clear Plexiglas™ table can also be used as a light table.

Scissors

As with all your tools, buy the best scissors you can afford. I recommend a sharp bent-handle 7" blade for general cutting. A small pair of dual handle scissors are handy for trimming and cutting at the sewing machine and for hand work. Snips are helpful to cut all those loose threads.

Rotary Cutter

Olfa® small, large or extra large size is a durable cutter. Use the small cutter to cut a single layer of fabric. Fiskars® rotary cutter is a good choice for those who have carpal tunnel syndrome.

Cutting Mat and Ruler

The cutting mat is made of self-healing vinyl. You must use a cutting mat with the rotary cutter. Olfa is a long-lasting brand. The most useful size is the large 24" by 36" mat.

Use any of the ruled and gridded non-flexible Plexiglas cutting guides as rulers. The Omnigrid® is marked with colors that show on light and dark fabrics. Do not use a wood or plastic ruler with the rotary cutter.

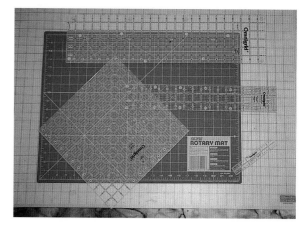

Iron

Use a clean, heavy steam iron for pressing the blocks. Use a dry iron to press the strips from the front. Using a steam iron may stretch the strips more than a dry iron. Press, do not push, when ironing. I use the Euro Pro™ or Rowenta® professional ironing system to press the blocks flat. I also use the steam and suction bed to block the quilt before and after binding.

Spray Starch

Use a liquid starch in a spray bottle to add sizing. Dampen, then iron the block.

Batting

Use thin ($1/4$" or less) cotton or cotton/ polyester blend batting or cotton flannel if you are going to machine quilt. Use a low-loft ($1/2$") polyester batting if you are going to hand quilt or tie. You can make a crazy quilt coverlet or wallhanging without batting.

Pins

Small, fine, glass-head pins are good for pinning seams. Use the $2^1/2$" long, large glass-head pins for pinning through several layers and batting.

Quilter's Basting Tacker

This hand-held gun-like tool with a fine steel point and short, $1/4$" nylon barbs is used to baste or tack the quilt layers together.

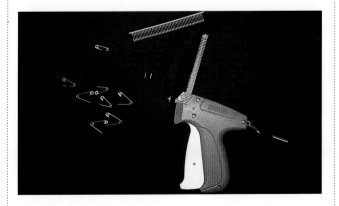

Safety pins

Size 0 or 1 safety pins may be used to pin baste the quilt. Use the smaller pins for thin quilts. If the quilt is an inch thick, use size 1 or 2 safety pins.

Hand Needles

- Quilting: Betweens needle sizes 7 to 12
- Basting: Milliners or Darners needle sizes 3 to 9
- Hand Piecing and Hand Appliqué: Sharps needle sizes 9 and 10

Machine Needles

- Piecing: Schmetz Jeans needle size 70 or 80
- Machine Quilting: Jeans needle size 80 with 100% cotton thread, Jeans needle size 70 or 80 with monofilament or clear polyester thread, Schmetz Topstitch size 80 with metallic threads, Metafil needle size 80 with metallic threads

Feet

- $1/2$" wide piecing foot or single needle foot: For all machine piecing
- Darning foot: "No turn" straight-line quilting, and free-motion quilting

- Walking foot: Straight seam quilting, applying binding, and straight seam piecing on thick layers

Silicone Needle Treatment

Needle Release™ is used to lubricate the eye of the needle for hand and machine sewing and quilting. Inside a plastic bag is a piece of felt soaked with silicone. To lubricate a sewing machine needle, place the bag under the presser foot and sew a few stitches through the bag. The eye of the needle is now coated with silicone. This coating helps to keep the thread from shredding when it passes through the eye of the needle. Re-stitch through the bag every two or three hours of quilting, and when you begin quilting or change threads or needles. Use with all threads and needles, and especially when using metallic threads. I use it all the time.

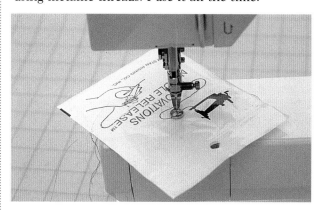

Threads

Use the best-quality 100 percent cotton thread you can find. Mettler 100% Cotton thread is one of the finest and strongest threads you can use. Machine piecing uses a lot of thread; but this is not the time to economize and use inexpensive threads. Some thread brands are not the fine quality you should use to be successful. The amount of time and effort you are spending deserves using a quality thread, and so does your sewing machine. "Linty" thread can ruin a machine faster than anything.

Mettler Metallic: The finest thread I have found. I can machine quilt an entire spool of thread without the thread breaking. Use the rayon embroidery threads for colorful machine quilting. Use the new machine quilting thread for a strong decorative stitch.

Mettler Cordonnet: A perle cotton-type thread used to sew on buttons or as a hand or machine top-stitch thread.

YLI®: Monofilament size .004. Clear or smoke color is used as a bobbin or top thread for machine quilting.

Mettler Embroidery: Very thin thread great to use as a bobbin thread or for hand appliqué.

Sulky®: Hundreds of decorative metallic and rayon threads that are suitable for creative stitching, embellishing, and machine quilting.

If you are sewing or quilting with a decorative thread and find it breaking, try a new needle, a different thread, or Needle Release, a thread lubricant. Even different colors within the same type of thread family may cause the tensions on the machine to vary. Or it may be your machine. When you sew, quilt, or stitch, make practice samples using different needles and different threads. Practice machine quilting on a patchwork block that includes seams, batting, and a backing.

There are new supplies and tools coming onto the market daily. Find out what is new and try them to find out what works best for you.

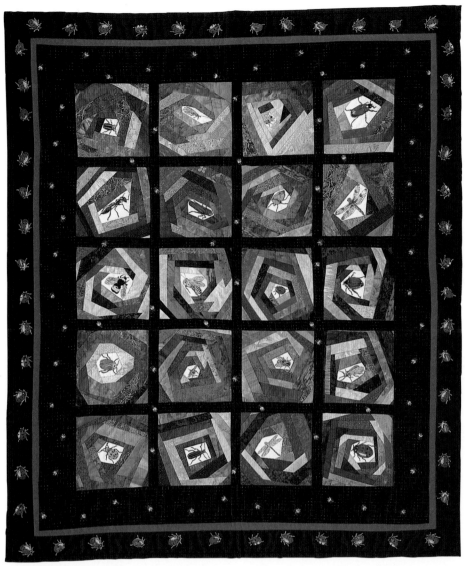

CRAZY ABOUT BUGS, 1996, 58" x 72", 9" block
Virginia Rojas
machine pieced, machine quilted, her first quilt

Planning A Cotton Crazy Quilt Top

A cotton crazy quilt makes a great gift for anyone. It is easy and fun to make and is a great quilt to use on a bed or wall. These quilts want to be seen. Because cotton crazy quilts are so easy to create, new quilters, including children, can make them. More advanced quilters can use the crazy quilt technique to design and create pieces to use in other projects. I am currently using a modified crazy piecing technique for a contemporary series of quilts. I have met many fabric artists around the world who are making fabulous quilts including the crazy piecing technique.

Study the variety of quilt styles pictured to get an idea of what you want to make as a first project. The quilt projects shown on pages 78-91 include the suggested yardage for the size shown. Crazy quilts can be addictive; one leads to another, and another. But for now, just start with one and let your imagination have full rein.

Sports

Weddings

Dinosaurs

Birthdays

THEME IDEAS

sports

family

wedding

anniversary

friendship

birthday

holiday

religious ceremonies

animals

music

hobbies

children

CHILDREN

BOATS

HOLIDAYS

SCHOOL

TROPICAL VACATION

WESTERN

CHOOSING YOUR FABRICS

The cotton crazy quilt eats fabric. You will need a lot, use a lot, and have a lot left over. My suggestion is to have a wide variety of fabrics from which to choose. More is better, and you will be very happy when you are sewing the quilt and don't have to run to the store and buy more. Any leftover fabrics can always be used for the quilt back or to start another project. Select fabrics you love; you will enjoy working with them, look forward to making the quilt, and want to finish the project as soon as possible. I suggest using 100 percent cotton fabrics for your first crazy quilt. They are the easiest to work with and give wonderful results. When you are more experienced and comfortable with different fibers and the qualities unique to each of them, try mixing and matching different types of materials.

If you need help selecting fabric, the quilt shop staff knows their stock and should be able to advise you on its availability. Don't hesitate to request something special. The shop owner will know what new prints are coming in, what is still available for special order, and what is no longer in print. This could be important if you are planning to use one particular fabric for the main theme. If the fabric is current and plentiful, you won't have a problem, but if it's the end of a bolt that can no longer be ordered, you will need to become a scrap quilt artist by changing fabrics and adding some new ones. The cotton crazy quilt is designed to use scraps, so you can easily substitute fabrics if necessary.

Decide on a theme before you begin selecting fabrics. Keep in mind the theme or message you want your audience to see. There are as many different themes as there are quilt ideas and people to make them for. A young man, Dale Kerlee, recently brought his finished quilt into The Quilting Bee. He had used discarded flannel shirts that had belonged to his father. This quilt is truly a storyteller that documents a part of his family's history and reminds them of the important part their father played in their lives and, ultimately, the lives of his descendants. What a treasure Dale has created for his family.

Most of the quilts in this book were based on a theme—some particularly memorable story the maker wanted to share. The theme fabrics are the main storytelling areas and are featured in the centers of the blocks. This fabric may be the largest print, or just your favorite fabric. One or more theme fabrics may be selected for the centers. The fabrics used in the center pieces should have a strong contrast between the print design and the background color or value of the print.

The strips should contrast in value or color when placed next to the center fabric. This contrast will separate and add focus to the center fabric. Select twenty percent of the strips to contrast with the center. The rest of the strips can be any value. Find as many fabrics that relate to the theme fabrics as you can for the strips. Don't worry about using different styles or colors together. You may want your theme quilt to have a scrapbook appearance. A theme crazy quilt is a great excuse to use as many fabrics as you can find. Don't worry that the combination may look a bit busy. That is, after all, what the crazy quilt is all about.

Once you begin the selection process, you will discover you are much more capable of selecting fabrics than you first realized. Select fabrics that appeal to you and use your instincts. If you like that first one, choosing coordinating fabrics will become easier and your search will become an adventure, and your fun has just begun.

PRIMARY FROGS, 1994
36" x 36", 7" block
Kathy Galos
machine pieced, machine quilted
Collection of Penny Nii

A frog print was the inspiration for this little quilt. The rest of the fabrics were chosen to add the variety of color and texture. Kathy chose not to use any other picture prints around the theme fabric so the frog print would be showcased. The four-sided center filler blocks give the quilt a Log Cabin look. The borders were made by sewing long leftover strips from the blocks, and then slicing them into narrow pieces. Fan-like, strip pieced blocks were used to turn the corners on the borders.

If you choose prints that use primary colors or pure rich colors, the quilt will appear bright, cheerful, and perhaps childlike. Soft florals enhance a traditional setting and add a restful, pleasant, and mature look. Choose from the hundreds of available "conversationals," or current pictorial storytelling fabrics to make your quilt a memory quilt.

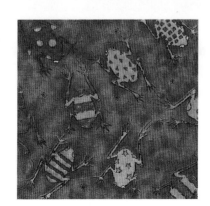

35

FLORAL FANTASY, 1995
54" x 54", 13" block
Roberta Bloom
machine pieced, machine
tacked

This wall quilt was inspired
by the wide variety of floral
fabrics available, and the
challenge of making a quilt
in the crazy style, which
was very new to this traditional quiltmaker. Roberta
machine tacked the layers
of the quilt together using
invisible nylon thread.

Contrast

When making a cotton crazy quilt you will use value, color, or print scale to show contrast between the strips and the center theme print design. You can add more or less contrast by your application of these elements.

Fabrics printed with designs of high contrast in value and scale are active and bold, and the designs are easy to see in the fabric. Prints with high contrast between the print design and the background color or value are good to use in the block's center. The center print designs may have more background showing between the print design and the first sewn strips. The contrast of the value or color of the background will help showcase the theme fabric.

To achieve a calmer and more neutral quilt, use fabrics printed with designs with low contrast in value and similar scale. When prints of similar value or scale are placed next to each other or next to the center, they will blend with each other and become a unit. If you want a low contrast, nondescript center, use strips with values similar to each other and the center fabric.

High contrast, light center, medium and dark value strips

Medium contrast, dark center, medium value strips, directional piecing

Medium contrast crazy pieced background, medium value pieced fan

DINOSAURS AND SUNFLOWERS
1994, 42" x 56", 14" block
Kathy Galos
machine pieced and machine
quilted

Do all young boys go through
the age of the dinosaur?
Kathy's son did, and was the
lucky recipient of this quilt.
This great dinosaur print just
happened along and found
its way into Kathy's creative
sewing basket. You can see
how the cotton crazy quilt is
a perfect way to showcase
the other wonderful fabrics
in the quilt and, because it is
so fast and easy to make it is
an ideal quilt to give to a
youngster to use and enjoy.

Value Contrast

Value contrast is the relationship between the light and dark. This contrast is relative and is determined when one value is placed next to another. To determine the placement of your contrasting fabric strips you will need to decide the look you want to achieve. Do you want to create a subtle or bold frame around the center fabric?

In Kathy's dinosaur quilt you can see the ultimate in planning the subtle strip contrast next to the centers. The contrast radiates from dark to light working out from the first strip that is placed next to the center. This is important if you want to add subtle contrast, feature the center, and are using a variety of busy multicolored strips.

ELVIS LIVE, 1994
54" x 54", 13" block
Diana Leone
machine pieced,
machine stipple quilted
using Mettler silver
thread

Elvis returns, in fabric.
The 1994 printing of
the Elvis fabric inspired
this quilt. The quilt is
dated to the year the
fabric was printed.

To achieve a more pronounced contrast, the centers in the Elvis quilt above are purposely framed with a high contrast color strip next to the center. This was done because of the limited color and value variations available in the fabric selection. The challenge was to set the center theme fabrics apart from the black strip fabrics. Red lamé was used to add contrast and frame the centers. The piano fabric came from a panel print. Tricot lamé fabric with lightweight fusible interfacing fused to the wrong side, was sewn to the corners of each block to create stars. This sets the blocks apart and added the glitz required for an Elvis quilt.

Value Contrast

Medium-light value strips sewn next to a dark background center

Dark value strips sewn next to a light background center

Strip colors coordinate with the bug print.
Medium-dark value strips sewn next to a light background center

Use color differences to create contrast.
Medium value strips sewn next to a dark center background

Scale Contrast

Scale contrast is the relationship between the size of one print and another. Scale is also relative. A small print may appear medium size when placed next to a smaller one. Use a small print next to a large print to contrast and add focus to the large print. The small prints can also act as "neutral" prints.

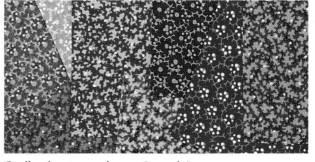

Small scale prints can become "neutrals."

Neutrals

Green is nature's neutral; leaves, grass, and trees become the background to showcase the brilliance of the bright colors of a garden. Greens and browns are used in printed fabrics to create neutral areas. Gold over-printing on fabric can also produce a browned or neutral area. Neutrals, in color mixing, are made by combining two colors that are positioned opposite each other on the color wheel. Any two opposites, such as red and green, will produce a neutral brown color. The neutrals are used to give the eye a resting place and to direct more attention to the theme prints.

Many different styles of prints and/or colors can become neutral fabrics. Neutral fabrics may be small texture-prints, plaids, checks, dots, color on color, or low-contrast prints. Any color small print that seems to rest or become passive when placed next to another print can be described as a neutral. Using neutral prints next to an active center design will calm the design and actually bring more focus to the center.

Center fabric with high-contrast background and dark neutral strips

Low-contrast print next to medium-contrast prints produce a soft one-value appearance. Tone on tone prints become neutrals

Center print with neutral strips

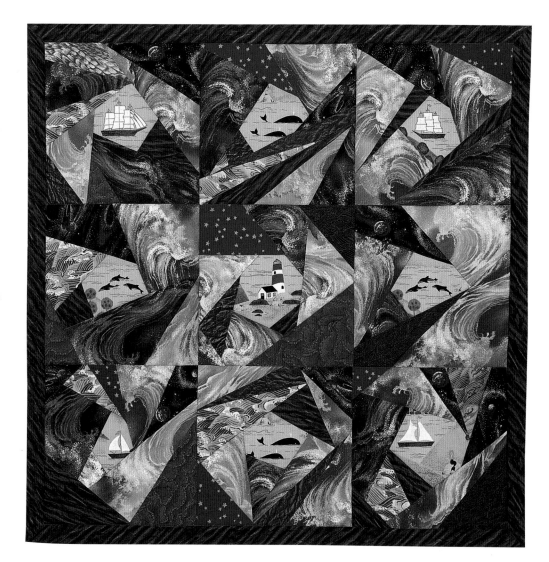

MESSIN' ABOUT WITH BOATS
1994, 41" x 41", 12" block
Diana Shaper
machine pieced, hand quilted

Diana used a nautical theme for this crazy quilt. One fabric was used for all of the center sections. The larger-than-normal strips of wave and sky fabrics were used to showcase the print and emphasize the theme. The crazy quilt center fabrics were placed vertically top to bottom. Sewing the strips around in a circle from the center out and maintaining the top and bottom of these fabrics was an added challenge.

Color Schemes

There are several things to consider when choosing a color scheme. Selecting a theme print in one color family may narrow your choice of coordinating print fabrics and help you decide on the rest of the colors to use. If you use a wide variety of theme prints, you will be able to select an even broader range of colors for the strips. Select fabrics that follow the theme and add focus to the center theme print. If you want the finished quilt to have a predominant color, use that color fabric for the sashing and/or border.

If you are decorating with a particular color scheme in mind, you may want to coordinate the fabric rather than mixing a lot of different patterns and colors. It will be easier to coordinate a color scheme when you choose the fabrics with color in mind first, then let the theme fall into place. Floral prints are easy to use in a harmonious, coordinated color scheme because there is a large variety of coordinated floral fabrics readily available.

There are as many beautiful color combinations as one can imagine. For now it is important that you begin with fabrics you like. Select your first fabric. It should be one you just love. Choose more fabrics to go with this first one, but don't over-coordinate them. Just have fun.

THE CRAZY QUILT PROCESS

The cotton crazy quilt is made up of a number of strip pieced blocks. The blocks, or squares, consist of a center piece of fabric that has from three to seven or more sides. Fabric strips are sewn to this center shape one at a time, onto a fabric foundation square, in a counter clockwise rotation. The foundation is completely covered with the strips of fabric. The blocks are all trimmed to the same size and sewn together with or without sashing. Borders may or may not be added before the quilt is layered and finished.

As with any project, there are a few guidelines that make the process a little easier. The following is an overview of these guidelines. For detailed step-by-step instructions see Let's Make a Quilt Top chapter, beginning on page 48, and Finishing the Quilt chapter, beginning on page 64.

Planning the Quilt Size

Your quilt can be made for a bed or to decorate an office wall. If the quilt is being planned for a bed, select your quilt size from the bed measurements shown. Note the measurements of the top of the bed. Decide how far you want the quilt to hang over the sides of the bed and add these measurements to the dimensions of the top of the bed. Make enough blocks to fill the entire size. Or, if you want borders, subtract the border measurements from the total quilt size. This measurement is the inner top size. Divide the inner top width measurement into equal block widths; for example, four blocks across that are 14" wide will make a inner top of 56", which will fit a double bed. Add the border widths to equal the entire quilt top measurement.

The easiest solution is to make 12", 14", or 16" blocks, sew them together, and add borders to make the quilt the size you want.

Standard bed	Quilt Top Without borders	Quilt Top With 10" borders
39" x 74" Twin	42" x 70" 14" blocks 3 by 5 blocks	62" x 90"
54" x 75" Double	56" x 84" 14" blocks 4 by 6 blocks	76" x 104"
60" x 80" Queen	70" x 84" 14" blocks 5 by 6 blocks	90" x 104"

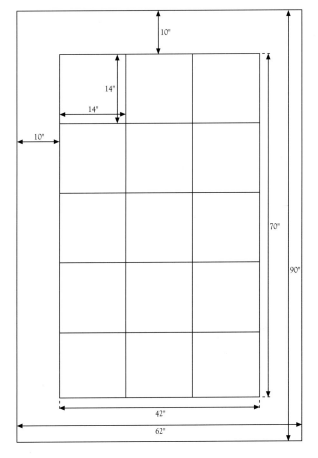

Twin size

EAGLES FOR ERWAN, 1996, 56" x 56", 14" block
Diana Leone
machine pieced, hand appliquéd, machine quilted

The eagle theme was chosen by Diana's thirteen-year-old grandson Erwan. The large scenic
eagle print was sewn to a sky fabric to frame and set the scene for the four medallion blocks.
The large eagles were cut from the fabric and hand appliquéd to the top before it was quilted.

Making Crazy Blocks

The size of the blocks in your quilt is up to you. The blocks used in the quilts in this book range from 4" to 16".

A ¹/₄" seam allowance is used when sewing the strips onto the foundation fabric. A ¹/₂" seam allowance is used when sewing the blocks together and adding the sashings and borders.

You can use any shape center with three to eight or more sides. Try not to cut any sides parallel. A three-sided center produces a pyramid or triangular appearance. A four-sided center will produce a more rectangular piece. If you want a Crazy Log Cabin block, cut a four-sided center. A five-sided center automatically creates a random crazy look and will be best for your first crazy quilt. The more sides you cut, and the smaller your centers are, the more strips you will need to sew. Use a large center for large blocks, and a small center for small blocks.

On page 92 you will find template patterns to use as guides for the centers. Practice cutting a few centers and you will see the many variations that will happen naturally due to designs in the fabric. You can use centers with the same or a different number of sides in the same quilt.

The center piece is cut and placed in the center of a lightweight cotton foundation fabric which is used to stabilize the sewing of the odd-shaped centers and angle-cut strips.

The strips are cut at a slight angle to achieve a more askew look. Keeping contrast in mind (page 37), select the strips at random and sew them from the center out in a clockwise circular rotation. Many of the quilts in this book use strips of fabric that are pieced with the print running a particular direction. *Messin' About with Boats* on page 42, and *Leone Pride* on the next page, are fine examples of this technique. It takes a little extra planning and may use more fabric than the suggested yardage, but the dramatic outcome will be well worth your time. The outcome can be quite dramatic.

The foundation fabric is filled past its edges. Piece the blocks until you have the number you need for your project. All the blocks within a quilt are trimmed to the same size after they are all sewn.

Place your blocks in the arrangement you desire and sew them together with or without sashing strips and borders.

Three-sided Center

Four-sided Center

 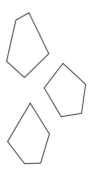

Five-sided Center

  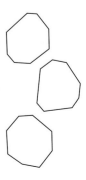

Six-sided Center

Eight-sided Center

THE LEONE PRIDE, 1995, 74" x 74", 14" block
Eddie Leone, Jr.
machine pieced, machine quilted, directional piecing

The Leone family, or "pride," is represented using different lion fabrics in the center of each square. The placement of fabric keeps the sky at the top and the earth below, with the jungle foliage placed vertically along the sides of the quilt blocks.

Sashing

Set the blocks together with or without sashing (divider strips) between the blocks. Sashing can be used to quiet a very busy quilt top, add a color, or make the top larger. Sashing can be any width that looks pleasing. Notice the sashing used on *Fruit Medley* on page 86 and *Crazy About Bugs* on page 31. Sashing may or may not include setting squares. Setting squares (optional) are small squares of fabric used to divide the sashing strips and add some color to the sashing.

Decide if there will be an outer row of sashing between the blocks and the border. Count how many strips (and setting squares) you will need. If you are not including setting squares, count how many short vertical sashing strips and how many long horizontal sashing strips you will need.

Decide how wide you want the sashing strips to be. The length of the sashing strips is equal to the size of the block. For example, you would use a 15" sashing strip for a 15" unfinished block. If the finished size of the sashing is to be 3" wide by 14" long, cut the strips 4" by 15" and the setting squares (optional) 4" by 4" to account for the $1/2$" seam allowances. If you are not including setting squares, you will measure and cut the long strips after the vertical sashing strips have been sewn to the blocks. Use scissors, or a rotary cutter, cutting ruler, and mat to cut the sashing and setting squares. Cut the long edge of the sashing on the lengthwise grain of the fabric. This will stabilize the blocks. Cut the number of strips needed.

Sew all of the vertical sashing strips to the sides of the blocks to form horizontal rows of blocks.

For detailed step-by-step instruction for adding sashing with setting squares see page 63.

Borders

Borders can be added, if you like. They can be simple or complex decorative additions to the quilt top; use one fabric or a combination. Notice the borders on *Primary Frogs* on page 35 and *African Dreams* on page 19. The width may be determined by the size you want your finished quilt to be, or the border can be any width that makes the inner top look balanced. Piece the borders or leave them plain. There is a lot of yardage used in the border, so use it to highlight the color or colors you want to feature. If you want a blue quilt, add a blue border.

Corner variation

If you want to add corner blocks to the borders, there are many options you can use: plain squares, pieced blocks, crazy pieced fan-shape squares, smaller crazy blocks to match the top's blocks, etc.

To determine the border length for the longest sides, measure the quilt top across the center parallel to the longest sides. Cut the borders from the lengthwise (parallel to the selvage) grain whenever possible. Cut the border strips the length measured above.

Follow the instructions for sewing with "match marks" on page 62 to pin and fit the borders to the inner top.

To determine the border length for the shortest sides, measure across the middle of the quilt top, including the borders, parallel to the short sides. Cut and add these shorter borders as you did for the longer borders.

Corner variation

TIP: I usually cut borders 10" wide and on the lengthwise (parallel to the selvage) grain. You will only need to purchase one length of fabric for the border. You can cut the four 10"-wide lengthwise borders from one 42"-wide piece of fabric. If the four borders are 12" wide or wider, you will need to purchase a second length of fabric or, piece the border using scraps. The fabric's lengthwise grain does not stretch, so the top's outer edges will stay straight and flat. Use the "match marks" on the border's edges to help align the inner top, easing the inner top's edges to fit the accurately marked and cut borders.

For instructions on finishing the quilt top, see Finishing the Quilt chapter, beginning on page 64.

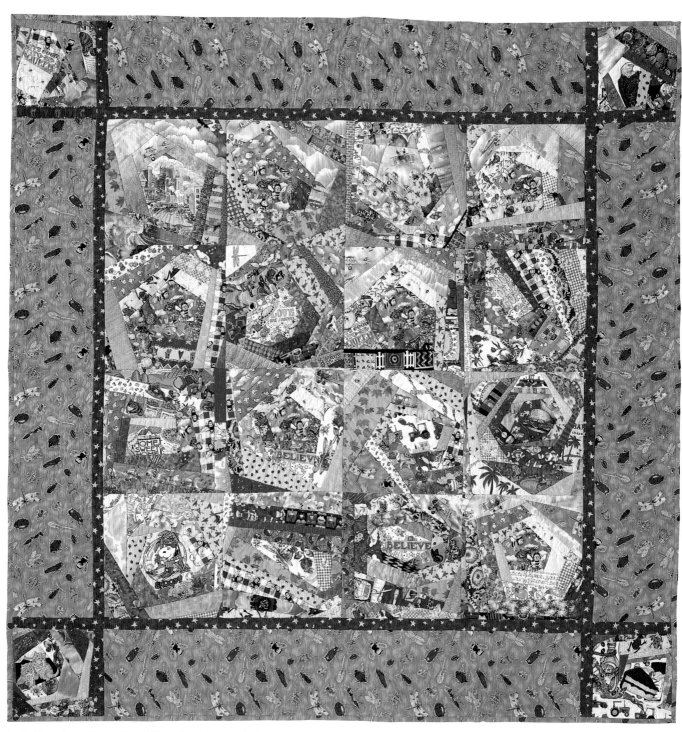

LET'S HAVE SOME CRAZY FUN, 1996, 80" x 80", 14" block
Diana Leone
machine pieced, machine quilted

Let's Make a Quilt Top

EQUIPMENT

template plastic

pencil or chalk marker

scissors

rotary cutter (optional)

cutting mat (optional)

cutting ruler (6" x 24")

measuring tape

thread

spray starch

iron

safety pins or basting tacker

sewing machine

YARDAGE REQUIREMENTS

		PILLOW (14" x 14")	WALLHANGING (51" x 51")	QUILT, page 48 (80" x 80")
	Components	1 block	4 blocks 3" sashing 2" inner border 8" border	16 blocks 1½" inner border 9" border 10" corner squares
	Foundation	16" x 16" or ½ yard	1 yard	4 yards
	Block Centers	7" x 7" or ¼ yard	½ yard	1 yard
	Strips	⅛ yard each of 10–20 fabrics	⅛ yard each of 10–30 fabrics	⅛ yard each of 40–60 fabrics
	Sashing Setting Square		½ yard 4" x 4"	
	Inner Border			1 yard
	Border		1½ yards	3 yards
	Backing	15" x 15" or ½ yard	2½ yards	5 yards
	Batting	14" x 14" pillow form or 1 lb. loose fill	60" x 60"	90" x 90"
	Binding		¾ yard	1½ yards

PILLOW (1 block) finished size 14" x 14"

WALLHANGING (4 blocks) finished size 51" x 51"

MAKING THE CRAZY BLOCKS

We will be using a 14" (finished size) block for the step-by-step instructions that follow. This is a great project to use those small scraps you have been saving. Construct the blocks using a ¹/₄" seam allowance. Children and beginning quilters should follow the scissor method of cutting.

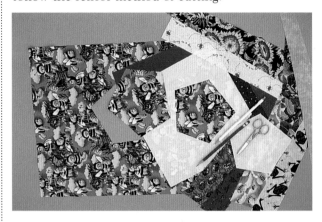

The Foundation Blocks

You can use any lightweight white cotton fabric for the foundation blocks. A cotton batiste or regular quilt cotton is fine. The foundation fabric blocks are cut 1" larger on each edge than the block's size; i.e., for a 14" finished block cut a square of foundation fabric 16" by 16". Cut sixteen foundation blocks 16" x 16" for the quilt, four blocks for the wallhanging, and one block for the pillow. Cut one additional foundation square 16" x 16" to use for the practice block.

NOTE: In 1985 Judith Baker Montano developed the Montano Method, a five-sided, center-piece technique for piecing traditional crazy quilts.

Cutting the Center Motifs

If you are a beginner, I recommend that you trace one of the shapes from page 92 onto template plastic and cut it out. Follow the scissor method for cutting fabric.

When cutting a center motif using a directional fabric (like a person—head on the top, feet on the bottom) place one of the points of the center shape on the top, not one of the straight edges.

It is best to use five-sided centers for your first crazy quilt blocks. After some practice you may be able to just look at the print area you want to use, take scissors or the rotary cutter, and cut shapes directly from the fabric. See the templates on page 92.

1 Choose the area of the fabric you want to see in the center of the block. Place the template onto this area of the fabric and mark around the template with a pencil (lead, white, or any color that will show).

✂ Scissor Method:

2 Cut the center out on the pencil line using scissors. Be careful not to cut into the center motif fabric.

WARNING: Always slide the safety cover over the blade when it is not in use. The blade is very sharp—use the cutter carefully. Be sure to keep the cutter out of the reach of children. To safely make the first cut, leave the safety cover closed over the blade until it is placed next to the ruler's edge. Then pull the safety cover back away from the blade and make the cut. Push the safety cover back over the blade after every cut.

✑ Rotary Cutter Method:

2 Use a rotary cutter, mat, and cutting ruler to cut out the center. You can glue small squares of sandpaper on the back of the cutting ruler so it won't slip when you are cutting the fabric. Align the cutting ruler on the inside of the pencil line so you won't cut into the center fabric. Place your left hand firmly on the ruler, but away from the edge. Place the blade of the rotary cutter next to the cutting ruler's edge. Draw back the safety cover on the rotary cutter. Cut the five sides of the center on the pencil line. You will need to rotate the mat so the next side of the center to be cut is in front of you and you are always cutting away from your body.

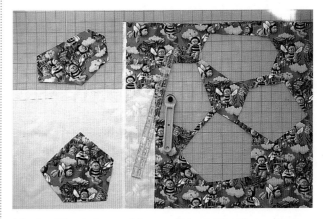

Note: The leftover fabric will look like Swiss cheese.

Cutting the Strips

You will be using strips that are cut at a slight angle. Strips that are cut with parallel edges will not create a random crazy effect. The fabrics are folded in half from selvage to selvage. The angled strips for this large block are cut $1^1/2"$–$2"$ wide at one end and $3"$–$3^1/2"$ wide at the other end. The length of the strips vary depending on the width of the fabric (4" to 22"). Use smaller centers and narrower strips when piecing smaller blocks and larger centers and wider strips for larger blocks. Kids can use wider strips. The strips should be a minimum of 14" long. If the 42" wide fabric is cut doubled, the strips will be approximately 20" long.

Use scissors, a ruler and pencil, or a rotary cutter, mat, and cutting ruler to cut the strips. If you are using a rotary cutter, the mat and cutting ruler have guide lines printed on them. Using these guide lines will make your work faster, easier, and more accurate.

✂ Scissor Method:

1 Fold one piece of fabric (approximately 42") in half, selvage to selvage. With the folded edge toward you, mark one piece of fabric at a time using a ruler and pencil. Mark and trim off the raw edges on one side of the fabric.

2 Angle the ruler to measure $3"$–$3^1/2"$ wide at the top selvage edge and $1^1/2"$–$2"$ wide at the bottom folded edge. Mark a line with the pencil. Cut on the marked line.

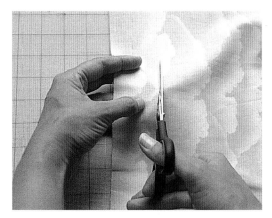

3 Move the ruler over to measure $1^1/2"$–$2"$ wide at the top and $3"$–$3^1/2"$ wide at the bottom and mark with a pencil. Cut two or more strips from each of the fabrics, alternating the angle of the ruler when marking the strips.

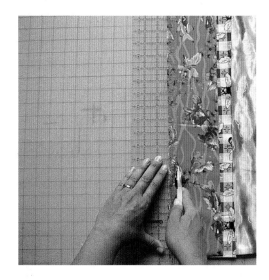

4 Cut the folds and the selvages off the strips.

✐ Rotary Cutter Method:

1 If you are using a rotary cutter, fold the fabrics (approximately 42" wide) in half, selvage to selvage. Place the folded widths of fabric on the cutting mat with the folded edges toward you. Align all the folded edges and the selvage edges on top of each other. Begin with two or three fabrics. It doesn't matter if the fabrics are different widths or lengths. Place the narrower pieces on top of the pile.

If you are right-handed, the raw edges to be cut off are on your left. This cut will make the edges even. Place the cutting ruler approximately 1/2" to 1" over the raw edges on the left side of the fabrics. Align the cutting guide on top of the cutting mat's guide lines.

Place your left hand on the cutting ruler, away from from the edge of the cutting ruler. Draw back the safety cover of the rotary cutter. Begin cutting at the bottom of the cutting guide. Press firmly on both the cutting guide and rotary cutter. Keep your hand alongside the cutter when you are cutting. Cut a few inches, move your hand up the cutting ruler, press on the ruler firmly, and cut a few more inches. Continue moving your hand up the cutting guide next to the rotary cutter as you continue cutting. This style of cutting will make it easier for you to cut through the layers because you are pressing down firmly on the cutting ruler next to the cutter and making short, firm cuts. Do not cut toward your body. Do not cut back and forth. Push the safety cover over the blade after every cut.

3 Cut more angled strips by moving the cutting ruler over to measure 11/2"–2" wide at the top and 3"–31/2" wide at the bottom. Cut two or more strips from all of the fabrics, alternating the angle of the ruler.

4 Cut the folds and selvages off the strips.

A crazy quilt uses a lot more fabric than you think possible. If you are prepared with a lot of fabric cut into strips and ready to sew, you will have more choices and won't have to stop to cut more. As you sew you will quickly see if the colors, values, and print designs are working. You don't have to use all the fabrics you've selected, and you can always add a few more if you need to. Now is the time to begin the practice block.

2 To cut the angled strips, place the cutting guide over the layered fabric. Angle the ruler to measure 3"–31/2" wide at the top and 11/2"–2" wide at the bottom folded edge. Cut the first angled strips.

Sewing the Blocks—Ready, Set, Go!

"Free and easy," "creative," "fast," and "addicting, I want to make more"—These are just a few comments students have exclaimed when they have sewn some blocks.

If you are planning to contrast the strips next to the center to help give the center definition, you need to think about that now. Refer back to the section that describes color, value, and scale contrast beginning on page 37. My advice is: Sew the remaining strips with random abandon. If the strips are well coordinated to begin with, you should be able to use almost any strip, at any time.

The first block is always the hardest. Just get started. It can be your practice block. Make all the trial and error in this block. Select the first strip, sew it to the center, select a second strip, and continue adding strips. You'll learn more about which fabrics will work and how to sew on the first block by just doing it. You can choose more carefully on the next block.

1 Arrange the strips in piles next to you at the sewing machine. Separate the strips into groups of different values; lights, mediums, and darks. The strips usually become a large mixed-up pile, so do not try too hard to keep the strips in order.

2 Place a center motif in the center of the foundation block, right side up. Place two pins in the center.

3 Select the first strip. Lay the strip on the side below or above the longest edge of the center motif. Note the contrast between the center and strip fabrics.

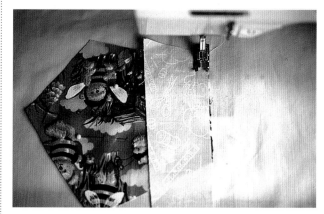

4 Place the strip face down over the center motif with the edges aligned. Be generous; leave 1" or so of extra strip fabric at the top edge. Sew the seam using a 1/4" seam allowance. Stop at the edge of the center fabric. Do not sew beyond the center's edges. Do not backstitch.

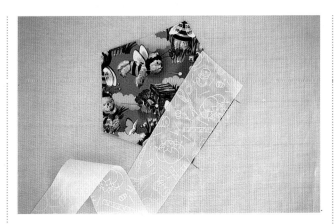

TIP: If you can't see where to stop and start stitching, lift up the edge of the top strip to see the fabric underneath and mark short pencil lines that correspond with the edges on the foundation fabric. Sew the strip from edge to edge or mark to mark.

6 Turn the block counter-clockwise. Place a second strip face down over the first strip and the center's edge. Sew from the top edge of the first strip to the bottom edge of the center motif.

5 Open the strip. Use an iron and press each seam open as it is sewn. You will be very pleased with the result if you press. Use a spray starch when pressing the strips. Overcut the strip fabric $1/2"$ longer than the edges of the center. Do not undercut the ends. Cut both ends of the strip fabric following the angles of the center piece.

7 Open the strip, press, and trim it $1/2"$ longer (overcut), and in line with the angles of the edges.

8 Repeat to add the third strip.

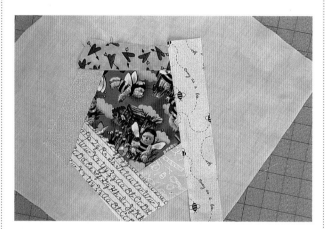

9 Repeat to add the fourth and fifth strips. Press carefully and cut off the loose threads.

10 Continue adding strips around the center.

11 Continue turning the block counter-clockwise, sewing strips around the center until the foundation fabric is more than filled. If there is no foundation fabric under the end of a strip, that is fine, but all edges of the foundation fabric must be completely covered. The foundation fabric is only used as a base or stabilizer to get you started. You have just finished your first block. Do not trim the block yet.

12 Sew all the blocks necessary for your chosen project. You will need sixteen blocks to make the quilt, four blocks to make the wallhanging, or one block to make the pillow.

The blocks may look misshapen. The foundation fabric may be crooked. The strips will extend past the foundation fabric. Do not trim any blocks until they are all sewn.

Tips, Observations, and Suggestions while sewing the blocks

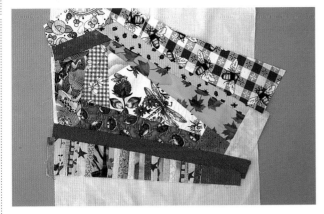

When the strips reach from edge to edge at one corner it is all right to fill in the corners with strips.

Select whatever print area within the strips that you like. You will have the same amount of scraps left over whether you use the middle or the end of the strip.

Use the wide end of the strip instead of the narrow end. The wide end will fill up large blank areas faster, especially when you get to the edges of the foundation fabric.

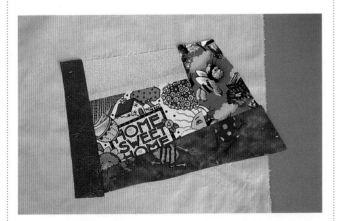

Are the angles changing direction? You can change the direction of the angle any time. Place and sew a strip over the area you want to change. You will never know what was under the new strip.

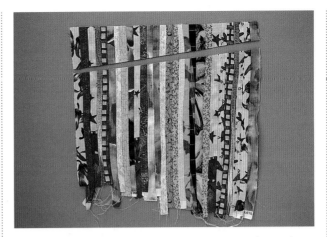

Need some variety? Sew some narrow ($1/2"$–$1^1/2"$) strips together to make pieced filler strips. Cut angled strips from this pieced fabric.

Are the sides getting too long? Sew a strip of pieced filler strip to add interest and variety.

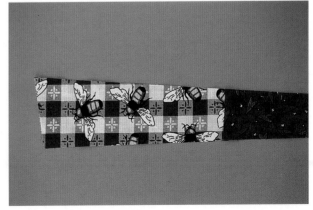

Are the strips or strip areas to be filled getting too long? Sew the two short ends of two different strips together to make a simple pieced strip. Use this pieced strip to add variety as a filler strip.

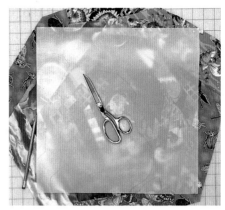

If any of the strips do not press flat, use sharp scissors to clip the foundation fabric and cut a slit in the foundation fabric. This will relax the strip and you can press the block flat.

Trimming the Blocks

Press all the blocks carefully before trimming the edges. Press from the back and from the front of the blocks. Use a liquid spray starch to add some body back into the fabric. The blocks will press flatter and will be easier to sew together.

It is very important to trim all the blocks to exactly the same size before assembling the quilt top. The blocks in this quilt are trimmed to 15" x 15" and will have a 14" x 14" finished size. (A $1/2$" seam allowance was added to each edge.) Note the block's size on a piece of paper, 15" x 15" trimmed size, 14" x 14" finished size. Careful measuring and trimming at this stage is very important. The blocks must be trimmed perfectly square and exactly the same size, but don't worry about the position of the foundation fabrics on the back of the blocks. Trim the blocks positioning the template where it looks best on the front of the block. Take your time and do a good job.

✂ Scissor Method:

1 Make a template out of cardboard or plastic, or use a large square cutting guide as a template.

2 Mark the block with the right side up by tracing around the template.

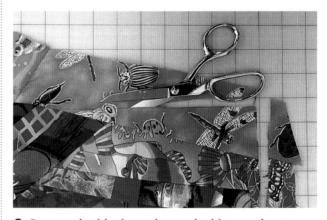

3 Cut out the block on the marked line with scissors.

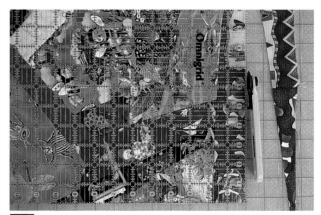

◢ Rotary Cutter Method:

1 Place the cutting guide on the front of the block. Align the cutting ruler with a line on the cutting mat. Trim off the uneven edges on the right-hand edge. Turn the block and align the top cut edge to a horizontal line on the cutting mat. Align the cutting ruler to a vertical line on the mat. Trim off the right-hand edge.

2 Turn the block. The first cut edge is now aligned on a vertical line. The line under the uncut edge should measure 15" to the left edge. Trim off the right-hand edge.

3 Turn the block the fourth time. Three edges should align with lines on the mat. Measure 15" from the left edge. Align the cutting guide on the 15" vertical line. Trim off the uneven edges on the right-hand edge.

Trim the remaining blocks to exactly the same size as the first block.

Instructions for finishing the pillow can be found on page 25.

To add sashing to the four-block wallhanging, follow the step-by-step instructions on page 63. Then proceed to Finishing the Quilt chapter, beginning on page 64.

ASSEMBLING THE QUILT TOP

Careful arranging, labeling, and sewing of the blocks will ensure the quilt top comes out flat and square. I use a $1/2$" seam allowance when sewing the blocks together, and adding sashings and borders. It is easier to sew and press the wider seam. This is different than the traditional $1/4$" seam used in most piecing instructions.

Arranging and Labeling the Blocks

Take a little extra time to come up with an arrangement you like. The cotton crazy quilt can look busy. You can include sashing strips to add one color and help calm the busy quilt.

1 Place the blocks on the floor or design wall. I use the Creative Grid™ (white flannel with a 2" grid printed on it) glued to a 40" x 60" sheet of foam core as a base on which to arrange the blocks. The fabric will stick to the flannel. You can move and arrange the blocks without pinning.

2 Arrange and label the blocks as indicated below. Write on the back of each block (on the foundation fabric) with a pencil, or pin a label on the back of each block. (R1-1, R1-2, R1-3, etc.)

Row 1 #1	Row 1 #2	Row 1 #3	Row 1 #4
Row 2 #1	Row 2 #2	Row 2 #3	Row 2 #4
Row 3 #1	Row 3 #2	Row 3 #3	Row 3 #4
Row 4 #1	Row 4 #2	Row 4 #3	Row 4 #4

3 Pin the blocks in numbered order on the design board and move the board next to the sewing machine.

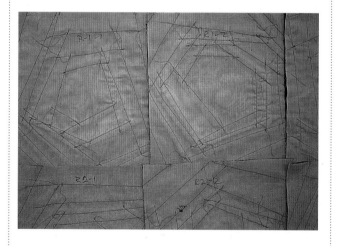

Sewing the Blocks Into Rows

Careful pinning and accurate sewing is important to ensure the blocks all match as you continue to assemble the quilt top.

1 Place block #2 over block #1 with the right sides together. Align the edges to be sewn and pin.

TIP: If you are right-handed, place the pins perpendicular to the edges of the fabric with the heads positioned on the right side so they can be removed easily as you stitch. If you are left-handed, place the pins perpendicular to the edges of the fabric with the heads positioned on the left side. Be sure the pin heads extend past the presser foot so they will be out of the way when stitching.

2 Use a $1/2$" seam allowance, a short stitch (10–12 stitches to the inch), and 100 percent cotton thread to sew a strong seam. To begin, backstitch 5–7 stitches to the edge and sew forward until you reach the opposite side of the block. Backstitch 5–7 stitches to secure the edge of the seam. The seam ends will be much stronger, stay straighter, and be easier to press open if you backstitch.

3 Continue sewing the blocks in order, to form the first horizontal row.

TIP: With the blocks right sides together, press the seam flat. Then open the blocks and press the seam open.

4 Press the seams open. Open seams will make matching the row seams easier. The open seams will also be easier to machine quilt.

5 Repeat to complete all rows.

Sewing the Rows Together

Continue to pin and sew accurately. Use my aligning pinning technique below to form a flat and square quilt top. Press the horizontal seams open as you finish sewing them.

1 Place rows 1 and 2 together with the right sides together.

2 To begin, place what I call an aligning pin (#1) into the first vertical open seam of rows 1 and 2, $1/2$" in from the edge. Push the pin straight down into the opened seam line of the front and back blocks. This pin will align the two seamlines while you pin the seam securely on either side of the aligning pin. The aligning pin is removed after the seams are securely pinned.

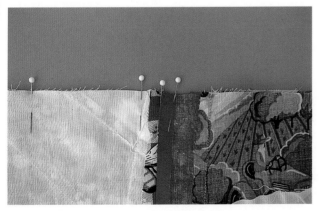

3 Place pin #2 into the seam allowance to the left of pin #1, holding the seam allowance open. Pin through the seam allowance of the back blocks and back through the front, $1/2$" from the edge. Place pin #3 to the right of pin #1.

4 Remove the aligning pin (#1).

5 Pin all the horizontal seams in the same way.

6 Pull or ease the blocks, if needed, to fit from pin to pin.

7 Place more pins along the seam edge. Pin every 1"–2" along the seamline to hold the edges together.

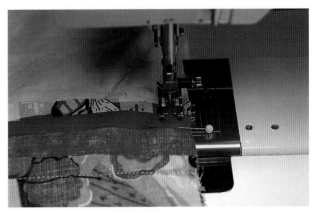

8 Sew rows 1 and 2 together using a $1/2$" seam allowance and pulling the seam slightly as you stitch to ease in any fullness.

9 Continue sewing the horizontal rows together using this process.

10 Press the seams open. Press the entire top on the front and the back.

Borders

Borders add interest to the quilt, as well as make it larger. This quilt has a narrow inner border and a wider outer border.

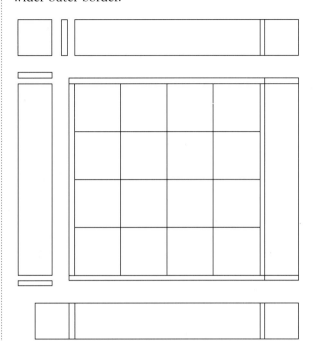

Adding Borders for Sixteen-Block Quilt

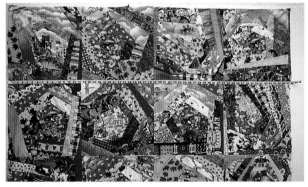

1 To determine the length of fabric you need for the border, measure the quilt top across the center from one side of the quilt to the other side of the quilt. Since this is a square quilt all four sides of the quilt are the same length.

2 Use scissors, or a rotary cutter, cutting ruler, and mat to cut the borders from the lengthwise (parallel to the selvage) grain whenever possible. Cut two inner border strips, the border length measurement (quilt top width) by 2½" wide (1½" finished) and four outer border strips, this measurement by 10" wide (9" finished).

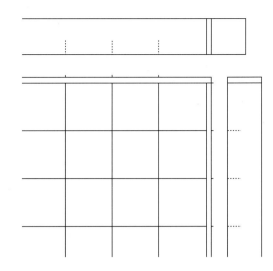

3 Use my marking method to make the quilt top come out flat and square. Mark the border edges exactly the measurement of the block edge from seamline to seamline. For example, if the blocks are finished 14" from seam to seam, mark the border edge at 14" intervals. Be sure to add a ½" seam at both ends of the border fabric to allow for the unsewn seams when marking the 14" intervals. When you pin the inner borders to the quilt top, the seamlines of the 14" blocks will "fit" into the 14" marks.

4 Sew the side inner borders to the quilt. Press the seams open or to one side.

5 Measure the quilt top across the center from the top of the quilt to the bottom of the quilt. Cut two strips this measurement by 2½" wide. Use the marking method above to pin and sew the top and bottom borders. Press.

6 Cut eight strips from the inner border fabric, 2½" x 10".

7 Sew one of these strips to each end of the four outer borders. Use the marking method above to pin and sew two of these outer borders to the side of the quilt. Press the seams open or to one side.

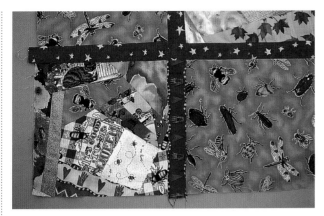

8 Cut four 10" corner squares and sew them to the ends of the two remaining border strips. Pin, sew, and press as in steps 3–5 to add the outer top and bottom borders.

Use this technique of marking for sashings, inner borders, borders, and even the binding, and you will have a perfectly square and flat top.

Adding Borders for Four-Block Wallhanging

Refer to the instructions on page 47 to add borders. Cut and sew the inner and outer borders onto the quilt top separately.

Optional Sashing for Four-Block Wallhanging

Use scissors, or a rotary cutter, cutting ruler, and mat to cut the sashing and setting squares. Cut the long edge of the sashing on the lengthwise grain of the fabric. This will stabilize the blocks.

1 Cut four sashing strips 4" wide (3" finished) by the size of your block (14"). Cut one setting square 4" x 4" from contrasting fabric.

2 Sew the vertical sashing strips to the sides of the blocks to form two horizontal rows of blocks. Press seams open or to one side.

3 Sew the setting square to the horizontal sashings.

4 Pin the horizontal sashing strip to the rows of blocks. Be sure to ease any fullness matching the seams to form a perfectly squared top.

5 Sew the rows together.

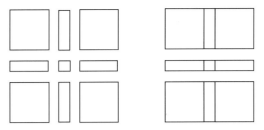

You have now completed your quilt top. Proceed to Finishing the Quilt chapter, beginning on page 64.

Optional Handle

To eliminate uneven and rippled edges caused by very dense machine quilting, sew a "handle" (strip of

fabric) to the edges of the quilt top before layering and basting. The handle is a 2"- to 3"-wide strip of any lightweight cotton fabric. This handle extends the quilt top and provides an area to sew into when you machine quilt. The edges will be quilted more evenly, because you will quilt right over the edges into the handle.

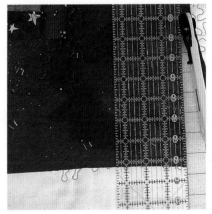

When the quilting is finished, the handle will be trimmed off when the quilt's raw edges are trimmed. Stay stitch $^1/_4$" from the edge, around the quilt.

Finishing the Quilt

BACKING

I like to have at least 3" of extra backing around the edges of the quilt top. The extra will ensure you have enough backing to cover the quilt top even if there is shifting during the finishing process. The excess will be trimmed off before the quilt is bound.

Most of the quilts in this book have pieced backs. Some are very elaborate and some are as simple as two or three strips sewn together. If you choose to piece the back, use any fabrics left over from the top, adding new fabrics as needed, to piece enough yardage to cover the back. Use rectangular pieces of fabric cut on the straight of the grainlines. Press the seams open. If you use scraps that have bias cut edges, the back will not sew together well or lay flat.

TIP: Decorate the back with photo transfers, write the story of the quilt on fabric, or add any embellishments you want to further personalize the quilt.

Some crazy quilts are made with the top and backing, and no batting, to be used as a wall decoration or as a "summer spread" or tablecloth. This type of quilt can be finished by sewing the top to the backing, right sides together. Leave a 10" to 15" opening on one side. Turn the quilt right side out. Hand stitch the opening closed. Tie or machine tack the quilt to hold the layers in place (see page 66). This "quilt" is ready to use.

BATTING

The pieced crazy quilt top is very stable and a little heavier than most quilt tops because of the use of the foundation fabric, so you may choose not to use any batting. If you do choose to use batting, use a thin (1/4" or less) flat cotton or cotton/polyester blend batting or cotton flannel if you are going to machine quilt. Use a low-loft (1/2") polyester batting if you are going to hand quilt or tie. I like to have at least 3" of extra batting around the edges.

Take the batting out of the bag and place it in a clothes dryer. Run the dryer on the "air" or "cool" setting for 5–10 minutes. You can put a large, dry towel in with the batt to help the batting "fluff." It will come out wrinkle free and beautiful. Do not put the dryer on hot or the batting might melt.

Alternatively, you can use a hair dryer to remove the wrinkles from the batting. Using the warm setting, hold the hair dryer 3"–4" above the batting, and watch the wrinkles smooth away.

Some batts need to be pre-shrunk. Read and follow the manufacturers directions before using these batts. I have found most battings made today are stable and good quality.

BASTING

It is easier to layer and baste the quilt on a large table than on the floor. You can place books or blocks of wood under the table legs to raise the table to a better height and position to work.

1 Leaving at least 2" of extra batting and backing around the edges of the quilt, layer the backing (wrong side up), a thin batting (optional), and the quilt top (right side up).

2 Place a cutting mat on the table, under the quilt section to be basted, so you will not damage the table.

There are three ways of basting the quilt layers together. You can use a Quilter's Basting Tacker, baste by hand using a long milliner's needle and thread, or use rust-proof safety pins to hold the layers together. Hand baste only if the quilt will be hand quilted.

I use the Quilter's Basting Tacker because it is fast and easy. I push the tack through the top, batting, and backing, and then up through the top. The tacks are tight and will hold the layers securely. (See the buyer's guide for information about ordering a tacker and scissors.) I can safely machine quilt over the tacks. This allows me to remove the tacks after the quilting has been completed. Be very careful when cutting the tacks to remove them. Do not cut the quilt fabric. There are scissors with a hook on the end to cut the tacks easily without harming the quilt. I used to worry about holes in the quilt from the barbs, but the new, fine needle tip and fine barbs do not harm the quilt. It is a great time saver.

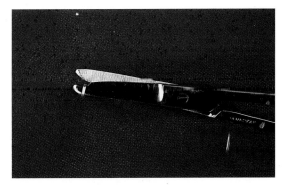

Use hooked scissors to safely cut the "stitch" of the tack.

As an alternative to hand basting or tacking, you can use size 0 or 1 rust-proof safety pins to pin the layers together. You will need 250–500 safety pins, depending on the size of the quilt. Note: If you use pins and are planning to machine quilt, be sure to remove the pins as you quilt so you won't damage the sewing machine or the needle.

3 Baste (tack or pin) every 3"–4". More basting will make the quilt easier to handle during the quilting process. It's easier to baste if you try to avoid the seams. Baste the part of the quilt that is on the table, on top of the cutting mat. As you finish basting a section, move the quilt and continue basting the portion of quilt that is on the table, on top of the cutting mat. Baste every 3" along the outer edges.

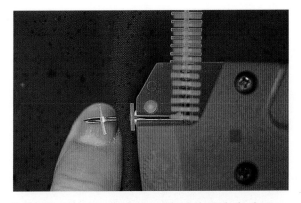

Push tack through to the back and back through the front

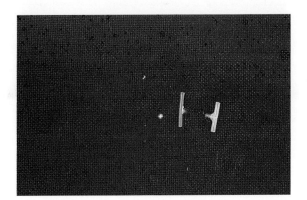

Tack shown from the front of the quilt

QUILTING

Decide if your cotton crazy quilt will be hand tied, straight-line machine, or free-motion quilted.

Since the quilt is pieced to a foundation fabric, the top is very sturdy and requires less quilting than some quilts. Deciding how to quilt your project depends on your comfort and experience level, time frame, and end use. Some people have time to hand quilt and enjoy the relaxation of the process. But, because of the additional thickness caused by the foundation fabric, hand quilting may not be the easiest choice for your cotton crazy quilt. I hand quilted for twenty years and wrote the book *Fine Hand Quilting*. I still enjoy hand quilting and appliqué, but I machine quilt most of my quilts. At this time of my life I just think about getting it done, soon and I thoroughly enjoy the machine quilting process. There are major trade-offs between hand and machine quilting and you should be aware of what they are. Read about both methods in *The New Sampler Quilt* book and *Fine Hand Quilting*. These books include thorough instructions, and give you the tools and materials needed to be successful. Or better yet, take a class in the method of your choice before tackling the project. See the Bibliography on page 95 for more hand and machine quilting books.

Machine or hand quilt in the major seamlines and around the motifs in the center pieces. Quilt some of the major strip seams. It is sufficient to quilt every 3"–5".

Tying

Tying a quilt is an easy way to assemble the quilt layers securely and quickly.

1 Pin the quilt on the front, using long strong pins with large heads to hold the layers together. Pin the major seam crossings. Place the pins in a pattern where you would like to see the ties or tacks. After the entire quilt is pinned, decide whether you will tie the quilt from the front, so the knots and tails will be on the front, or turn the quilt over and tie from the back, so the knots and tails will be on the back. For the ties, use strong perle cotton type thread such as Mettler Cordonnet or 3-ply washable yarn and a large-eyed yarn darning needle.

2 Push the needle in where the pin is, remove the pin, and push the tip through to the back. Push the tip up and into the back 1/4" from where the tip came through. Push the needle back out through the surface of the quilt. Pull the needle and yarn through the quilt layers, leaving a 3" tail of yarn. Use a rubber finger, or a balloon to help pull the needle through the layers.

3 The thread (or yarn) needs to be tied in a strong knot. A half knot with a half hitch, or a bollen knot, is strong and will not come untied. A square knot will untie.

4 Form a half knot (just like starting to tie your shoe) left over right.

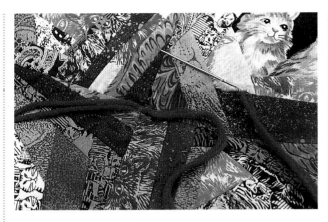

5 Pull it tight.

6 Hold the four strands of yarn in the left hand and the needle in the right hand. Make a circle around the strands in the left hand with the threaded needle.

7 Put the needle through the loop, pull the thread through. This forms a half hitch knot.

8 Tighten the half hitch down over the half knot.

9 Trim, leaving 1" tails.

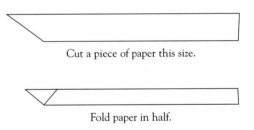

Cut a piece of paper this size.

Fold paper in half.

Tip: Magic Needle Threader

Cut a piece of paper the shape of the needle threader above. Fold the paper in half and lay the end of the yarn in the center of the fold. Hold the folded needle threader with the yarn inside and insert the needle threader in the eye of the needle. It works!

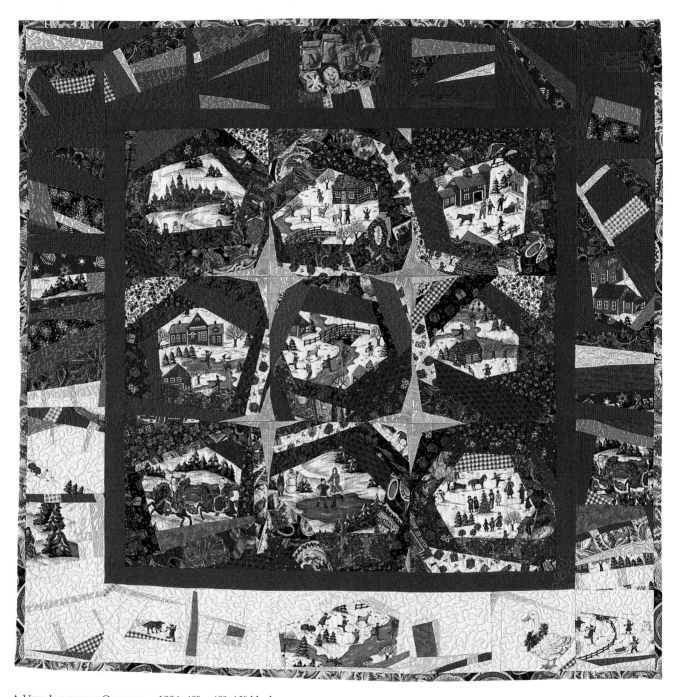

A Very Important Christmas, 1994, 48" x 48", 10" block
Diana Leone
machine pieced, machine stipple quilted using Mettler silver thread

The 1995 VIP® Christmas fabric line was used in this quilt. The border was pieced into blocks to create the sky and the effect of snow on the ground. Gold and silver lamé fabrics were pieced onto the corners of each block after they were trimmed to size. The lamé fabrics at the corners of the blocks create stars, which separate the blocks and act as a sashing.

Machine Quilting

The cotton crazy quilt is very stable and requires less quilting than the average quilt because the strips are sewn to a foundation fabric. Analyze the project to determine where you will place the quilting stitches. Your sewing machine must be clean and in excellent working order. For all straight-line quilting use a walking foot on your sewing machine so the quilt layers will feed through the machine evenly. For free-motion and stipple quilting you will lower the feed dogs of your sewing machine and use a darning foot. I always make a small sample using a left-over block that has been layered with batting and backing. See the Tools and Supplies chapter beginning on page 28.

1 Begin by setting all the machine tensions and pressure adjustments to the proper settings for normal sewing. Attach a walking foot.

Use a high quality 100 percent cotton thread such as Mettler for both the top and bobbin. You can more easily regulate and balance the tensions and sew the best stitch when the top and bobbin threads are the same fiber and weight. As you practice and become more experienced, try all the different decorative threads. Each different thread change will require adjustments to the tensions and pressures. Practice on a small sample to test your ability, threads, needles, and machine.

A large flat sewing surface is ideal when machine quilting a large quilt. The flat bed of the sewing machine should be lowered into the cabinet so that the sewing surface of the machine is flush with the surface of the cabinet. A Plexiglas® extension table can be ordered to fit most machines (see page 28). This is a great second choice if space is limited.

2 Quilt the long seamlines ("in the ditch") between the blocks, working from the seams closest to the center of the quilt out to the edges of the quilt. Then quilt some of the strip seamlines. Quilt enough to hold the quilt top, batting, and backing together securely.

Free-Motion and Stipple Quilting

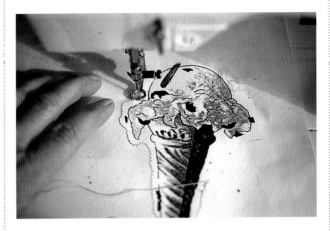

If you can write your name, you can learn how to hand-guide (free-motion) machine quilt. Practice by photocopying a piece of fabric onto paper. Sew the straight seamlines in a block, backwards, sideways, and forward without turning the quilt, by using "no turn" free-motion machine quilting. You will be hand guiding the quilt under the needle. The movement of your hands, fast or slow, will determine the length of the stitches.

Lower the feed dogs of your sewing machine and attach a darning foot. Sew with the needle stitching fairly fast, and move the fabric under the needle slowly and steadily. Your hand movements control the stitch length. Practice, practice, and then practice some more. Once you get the motion, timing, and quality you are looking for, you will be pleased with the outcome and enjoy the process.

Outline the center motifs and fill in the background of the blocks using free-motion stitching.

Stipple quilting is a gracefully meandering line of stitching that runs close to itself to fill an area, as shown in the border to the right.

TRIMMING THE QUILT

The edges of the quilt will need to be trimmed even and square. Place the quilt on a flat surface.

1 Measure the length and width of the quilt across the middle.

2 Mark the measurements of the finished size around all the edges with a straight edge and a pencil or chalk marker. Use these lines as a guide to trim the edges.

 Scissor Method:

3 Cut on the marked lines with scissors.

 Rotary Cutter Method:

3 Place the cutting mat under one corner. Place the cutting ruler on the marked line. Trim the edge using a rotary cutter and ruler. Move the mat and cutting guide and carefully cut the excess fabric from around the edges.

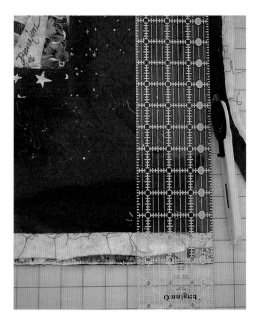

4 Machine stitch around the quilt ¹/4" from the edge. Use a long (4mm) stitch to ease any rippled edges flat before binding.

BINDING

Choose a binding fabric that will give your quilt the finished look you desire. The binding is the final frame. The fabric should blend with the border fabric. I like to use a double-fold binding and a $^3/8$" seam allowance. The finished binding is approximately $^1/2$" wide.

1 To make the binding, cut strips of coordinating fabrics $2^3/4$" wide on the lengthwise grain (parallel to the selvages) whenever possible. The binding will not stretch and will help the edges to stay flat and square. Piece enough lengths of the fabric strips together to go around the quilt plus an extra 10" to allow for the corners and finishing the ends. You will need approximately 10 yards for the quilt and 4 yards for the wallhanging.

Fold the binding in half, wrong sides together, and press.

2 Place one end of the binding along one edge of the quilt top about 10" up from a bottom corner, aligning the raw edge of the binding to the edge on the front of the quilt. Fold the end at a 45° angle.

3 Fold the binding edge over and align the raw edges. Pin a few pins at the beginning of the binding to hold it in place. Do not pin all of the binding to the quilt. You may need to ease the binding as you sew.

4 Begin the sewing 3" down from the folded end. Sew $^3/8$" in from the raw edges. This is a good time to use the walking foot. This foot is especially helpful when sewing thick layers together. The binding and quilt will feed through the sewing machine at the same time resulting in a nice, flat, even binding.

5 Stop stitching $^3/8$" from the edge. Backstitch. Turn the hand wheel of the sewing machine to lift the needle out of the fabric. Pull the quilt a few inches away from the needle. Turn the quilt one quarter counter-clockwise. Fold the binding straight up forming a 45° angle.

6 Fold the binding back down over the angle. The top folded edge must be even or slightly above the top quilt edge.

7 Stitch $^3/_8$" in from the edge beginning at the top edge. Continue to sew the binding around all the edges of the quilt, sewing the corners as in steps 5–6.

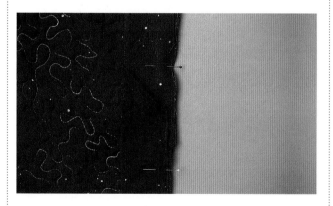

8 To finish the binding ends, place the unsewn end over the beginning (folded end) of the binding. Cut the end $^1/_2$" longer than the beginning edge and insert the unsewn, cut end into the folded edge of the binding.

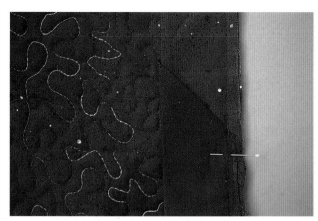

9 Pin and sew the seam across the overlapped ends to finish the seam.

10 Bring the folded edge of the binding around to the back of the quilt. Press the binding away from the quilt. Pin the folded edge of the binding to the back of the quilt. Tuck in the corners, forming a mitered corner on the front and the back.

11 Hand stitch the folded edge to the quilt back using a blind hem stitch.

OR

Sew the binding to the quilt entirely by machine. Use the previous method, except sew the raw edges of the binding to the back of the quilt first. Bring the folded edge to the front.

Topstitch by machine, using a straight or blanket stitch. Use matching thread as the top thread and invisible thread in the bobbin.

LABELING

Be sure to label your quilts. The recipient of the quilt, now or in the future, will be glad you did.

I like to machine quilt my name, the date, and the title of the quilt, into the quilt while I am machine quilting.

You can make great labels using the new computerized sewing machines.

Another option is to make a cloth label, write on it with a permanent felt pen, and sew the label to the back of the quilt. To stabilize the fabric for handwriting, iron freezer paper to the back of the fabric. When finished writing, pull off the paper and sew the label to the quilt. You can write the entire history of the quilt on fabric and attach this to the quilt.

Use your new computerized machine to create a personal label.

Handwrite your name on the back using a permanent pen.

Hand appliquéd label

Lettering printed on fabric directly from ink jet printer. Bugs fused to the label using HeatnBond®.

Labels on quilts have become very fun and creative. Design anything you want—just be sure to label the quilt.

DISPLAYING

The easiest and least expensive way to hang a quilt is to sew a sleeve on the top of the back.

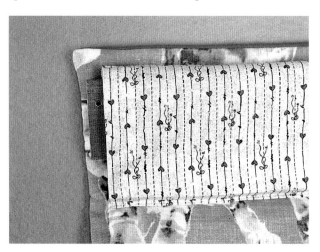

Cut long strips of coordinating fabric 9" wide by 42" long. Sew enough strips together to equal the width of the quilt. Trim this strip so its length matches the width of the quilt. Make a $1/2$" fold (to the wrong side of the fabric) on the two short ends of the sleeve and top stitch. Fold the strip in half lengthwise with the right sides out. Sew a seam along the long side, $1/2$" from the raw edges. Pin the sleeve to the back of the quilt with the seam folded to the back against the quilt back so the seam doesn't show. Align the seamline of the sleeve with the seamline of the binding. Hand stitch the sleeve to the quilt along the folded seam edge and along the bottom fold.

Use a $1/2$" x 2" piece of door molding to hang the quilt. Cut the molding length to equal the width of the quilt, minus $1/2$". Place the wood into the sleeve (the wood should peek out of the sleeve about $1/2$" on each side). Position the quilt on the wall where desired. Fold the edge of the quilt back slightly and nail the molding to the wall with small finishing nails.

There are many other options for hanging quilts. Beautiful wooden hangers can be made or purchased or decorative rods can be used to display your quilt.

Embellishment

The cotton crazy quilt provides a wonderful foundation to adorn with any of the current popular embellishment techniques. Add some photo transfers, pen writing, silk ribbons, charms, buttons, or any memorabilia you can think of to personalize the quilt.

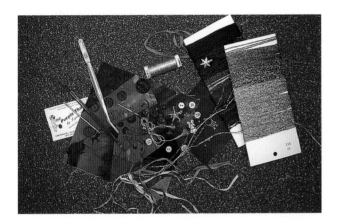

PHOTO TRANSFER

Select the photographs you wish to print on fabric. Group the photographs, separating the light ones from the dark ones, and the black and white from the color. Glue each grouping to a separate 8^1/$_2$" x 11" sheet of lightweight tagboard. Leave ^{1}/$_2$" space around each photo for the seam allowances and a place to cut the pictures apart.

Use a fine, tightly woven white or light-colored cotton fabric such as Kaufman's untreated Pimatex™ fabric. This fabric has no chemical treatment and will accept the transfer and detail of complex photographs.

Take the photos and fabric to a photo shop that can transfer photos onto fabric. They need to have a laser color copy machine and a heat transfer press. The shop should run a test sample for you and make corrections while you wait. To do this process at home, you will need to purchase Photo Effects™ paper. Make color laser copies and use an iron or flat press that will heat to 350°. See Buyer's Guide on page 96 to order photo transfer fabric and paper.

MEMORIES OF MY FATHER, 1994, 42" x 42"
14" block
Virginia King
machine pieced, machine quilted

Memories of a loved one can become pictorial scrapbook albums by using family photographs. Virginia selected some of her favorite photos and had them transferred to fabric. Excerpts from news articles about Virginia's father and personal letters between the two were transferred to some of the fabric used for the strips. The "solid print" fabrics radiate from light to dark tones, illuminating the photos. The use of silk ribbon roses adds a nostalgic touch.

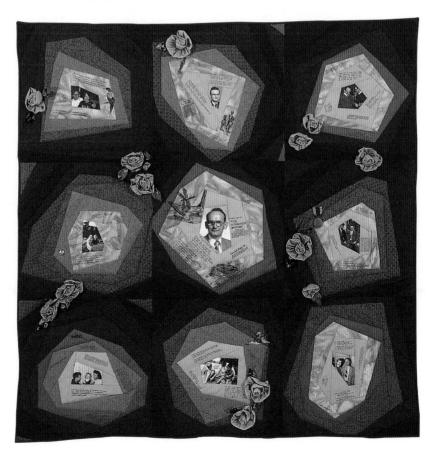

MUSIC AND CATS, 1994, 64" x 76", 12" block
Virginia Schnalle
machine pieced, machine embroidered, machine appliquéd cats,
photo transfer, and permanent felt pen writing

As the theme for her quilt, Virginia used the words of Albert Schweitzer, "There are two means of refuge from the miseries of life: music and cats." These words are depicted in the center of one block. Virginia's son, Wally Schnalle, is a talented musician who also loves cats, and Virginia had a wonderful time collecting all the fabrics that related to her theme. Some of the stitched and appliquéd centers represent song titles of Wally's compositions, and others represent his musical group. Also included is a graphic representation of him playing his drums. Photo transfer block centers represent his album covers. Virginia is an expert machine needle artist and she can draw with the sewing machine as well as someone using a pencil. A variety of threads were used to draw the stitched pictures.

BUTTONS, BEADS, AND MEMORABILIA

Use ribbons, buttons, and any memorabilia that will personalize your crazy quilt. Sew embellishments on by hand or machine. Mettler's Cordonnet topstitch thread can be used by machine or hand and will hold most objects securely. Use a monofilament thread if you do not want the thread to show.

Detail of Jacket on page 17. Buttons and silk ribbons sewn by machine with clear thread.

SILK RIBBON EMBROIDERY AND RIBBONS

You can use silk ribbon to make flowers, and add creative stitches to embellish your cotton crazy quilt. You will find silk ribbon easy to use, and the results are beautiful. Use ribbon to add dimension and interest to your project. Refer to the books in the bibliography for excellent ribbon embellishment instructions.

WRITING ON FABRIC

A variety of permanent felt markers are available from craft stores. The ultra fine Sharpie® and Sakura® pens come in a variety of line thicknesses and are easy to use. Micron® pens have very fine points and are good for detail drawing and writing. Use Dual Shader™ permanent blending brushes to achieve a watercolor technique. Be sure to test your markers on a scrap of fabric first. Write on the fabric, then iron and wash it to make sure you achieve the results you desire.

There are as many ways to adorn and add personal touches to the cotton crazy quilt as there are quilters to make them. This quilt provides a perfect surface to embellish. Use this opportunity to document the stories and enhance your memory quilt.

FABRIC PAINTING

Versatex is a water-soluble, non-toxic, easy to use paint. It is permanent on fabric when heat set by ironing. These paints can be mixed together and are easy for children and beginners, as well as advanced artists, to use. They are available in many colors and in starter sets. Apply the paint to fabric using brushes, your fingers, found objects, or any type of tool. Use Kaufman's Pimatex fabric or any tightly woven, fine, pre-washed 100 percent cotton fabric.

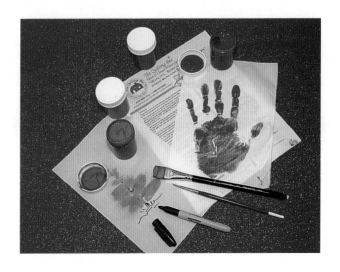

LIFE BEGINS AT FORTY, KATHY, 1994
Virginia Schnalle
machine pieced, machine quilted, thin cotton batting, photo
transfer, appliquéd prize-winning quilt ribbons, felt pen writing,
machine appliqué, free-motion stitchery

Life Begins At Forty, Kathy

QUILT SIZE: 54" x 64"

BLOCK SIZE: 10"

FABRICS

Centers: $1/8$ yard each of 10 different fabrics

Strips: 12" x 12" scraps or $1/8$ yard each of 18–20 different fabrics

Foundation: $2^3/8$ yards

Border: $1^3/4$ yards total of 3 different fabrics

Backing: $1/2$ yard each of 7 different fabrics (mostly scraps from the leftover front fabrics)

Binding: 1 yard

Batting: 60" x 72" thin cotton batting

Virginia made this quilt for her daughter, Kathy Galos, to commemorate Kathy's first forty years. Each block is a vignette of Kathy's life. She was a postal carrier, is a mom of very active sons, cooks (when she has to), goes to lots of sporting activities, loves to sew and quilt, and teaches all sorts of quilt-related classes, especially what is new and creative. Each of the twenty blocks has a theme.

This storytelling "theme within a theme" quilt is one of the best examples of using all the fabrics you can find that relate to the story being told. You may need to do some research to learn as much as you can about the person who will receive your quilt so the fabrics you use will be enjoyed by the recipient. You will then have the fun of searching for fabrics that relate to the person and the theme. As you look at the photograph of this quilt, note how different techniques and embellishments can be used to enhance your quilt.

10" block with 5-sided center

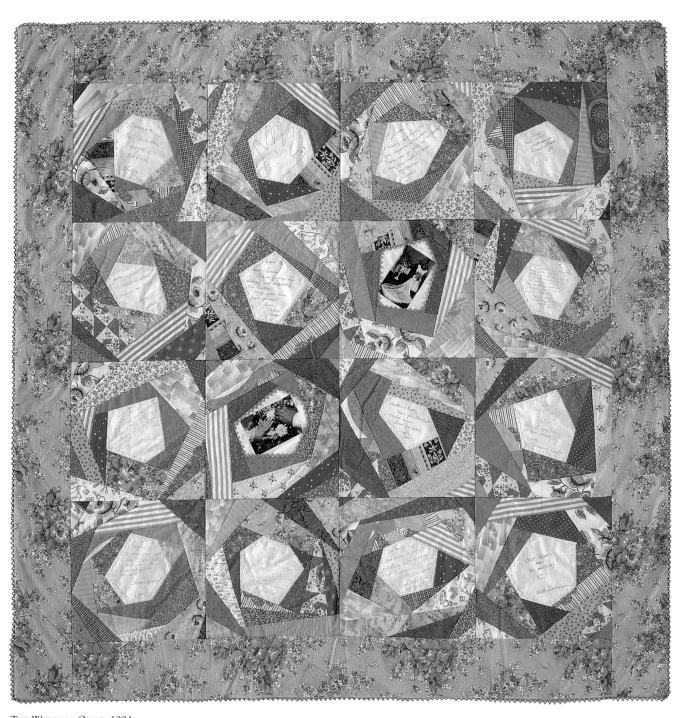

THE WEDDING QUILT, 1994
Meta Hodson
machine pieced, machine quilted, embroidered, felt pen, photo transfer

The Wedding Quilt

QUILT SIZE: 68" x 68"

BLOCK SIZE: 14"

FABRICS

Centers: 10" x 10" muslin squares or $1^{1}/4$ yard total

Strips: $^{1}/8$ yard each of 32 different prints or $^{7}/8$ yard total

Foundation: $3^{3}/4$ yards lightweight cotton

Border: $1^{3}/4$ yard

Backing: $4^{1}/4$ yards

Binding: $^{3}/4$ yard

Batting: 74" x 74" low-loft polyester

The cotton crazy quilt is a wonderful way to incorporate a variety of blocks to make a friendship quilt. The center muslin fabrics were distributed to a circle of friends who then embellished the muslin with embroidery, permanent felt markers, or in any way they wished. Two blocks included photo transfers. The blocks were then collected and arranged into the quilt top design. The strip fabrics were chosen to appeal to both the groom and the bride. This was a fast and easy quilt to make, and a meaningful project for both the participants and the happy couple.

14" block with 6-sided center, photo transfer

PLAID FLANNEL QUILT, 1996
Patrick Galos, age 12
machine pieced, hand tied, right sides sewn together,
turned right side out, hand tied at block corners

Plaid Flannel Quilt

QUILT SIZE: 56" x 70"

BLOCK SIZE: 14"

FABRICS

Centers: $1/2$ yard

Strips: $1/4$ yard each of 24 different fabrics

Borders: scraps from top fabrics or $1^3/4$ yards

Foundation: $2^3/4$ yards lightweight cotton

Backing: $3^1/2$ yards

Batting: 62" x 76" low-loft polyester or cotton

Plaid flannel is a favorite of young and old alike. Patrick likes to sew and wear his own shorts made of flannel, so naturally the next step was to make his own flannel quilt. Black was selected for the three-sided centers to contrast with the surrounding plaids. Finding light-colored flannel was especially challenging. This is a warm and snugly quilt, backed with a sports flannel fabric. This quilt was assembled using the easy no-binding technique, and hand tied with top stitch thread.

Easy No-Binding Technique (with batting): Cut the batt the same size as the backing and quilt top. Pin the top and backing right sides together and place this on top of the batt. Re-pin through the batt. Be sure the pins are on the top layer perpendicular to the edge. With the batt next to the feed dogs, sew around the edges $1/2$" from the edge. Leave an 8" opening. Turn right side out and poke the corners out with a chop stick, or similar tool. Press from the back. Pin the opening closed. Topstitch by machine or hand sew the opening closed.

14" block with 3-sided center

GRANDMA'S TEAPOTS, 1995
Mona Woo
machine pieced, hand appliquéd, right sides sewn together,
turned right side out, no batt, hand tied

Grandma's Teapots

QUILT SIZE: 41" x 41^1/$_2$"

BLOCK SIZE: 12"

FABRICS:

Strips and background: ^{1}/$_4$ yard each of 14 different fabrics

Foundation: 1^1/$_4$ yards

Teapot bodies: ^{3}/$_8$ yard each of 9 different fabrics

Teapot handles and spouts: ^{1}/$_8$ yard each of 9 different fabrics

Backing: 1^1/$_2$ yards

The pieced background squares add depth to *Grandma's Teapots*. Mona, who is an avid teapot collector, used 1940s bark cloth and original 1930s fabrics and flour sacks as the feature prints. The teapots were hand appliquéd onto the pieced fabric blocks, which were sewn to the foundation squares. Reproduction fabrics (87 fat quarters) were added to the outer edges of the blocks. The quilt was assembled using the easy no-binding technique (without batting) on page 25, steps 4–9.

See page 94 for teapot template.

12" block with appliqué on pieced background

Fruit Medley, 1995
Susie Uyeda
machine pieced, hand quilted

Fruit Medley

QUILT SIZE: 30" x 41"

BLOCK SIZE: $4^1/2$"

FABRICS

Centers: $^1/2$ yard

Strips: $^1/8$ yard each of 15 different fabrics

Foundation: $^3/4$ yard

Sashing: $^1/3$ yard

Setting squares: $^1/8$ yard

Border: 1 yard

Backing: $1^1/4$ yards

Binding: $^1/2$ yard

Batting: $1^1/4$ yards of cotton flannel

Susie is well known as a miniature dollmaker and teacher. This is her first quilt and notice, it is a miniature also.

This quilt is a visual treat. It is a medley of colors and shapes, as satisfying to the eyes as real fruit is to the palate. The challenge of creating a theme quilt is especially rewarding when, as in this quilt, you take scraps of materials, re-sew them, and make them into something completely different. Susie chose to use sashing with setting squares to separate the crazy patch blocks. As the fruit is the result of a seedling maturing to a tree, so the quilt begins with an idea, is nourished with love and creativity, and becomes the fruit of the quilter's needle.

$4^1/2$" block with 5-sided center

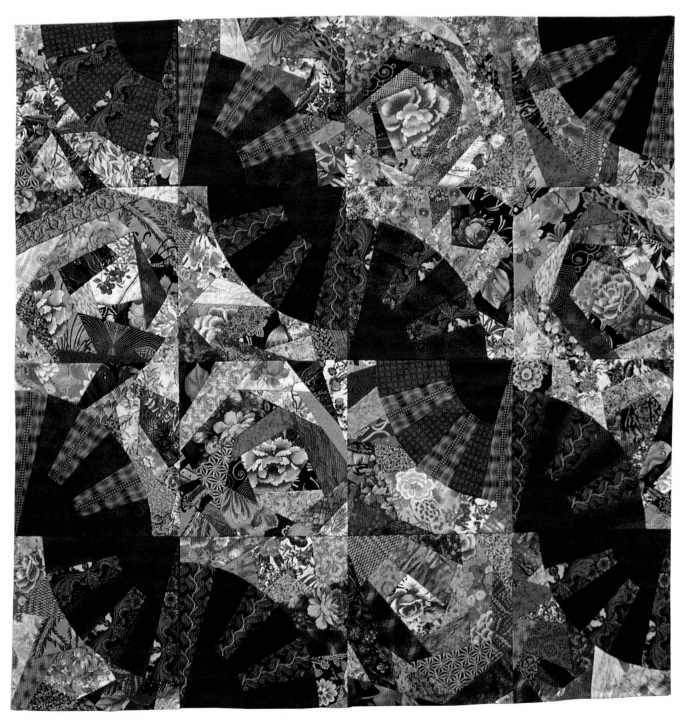

FAN LOVER, 1995
Mona Woo
machine pieced, hand appliquéd, machine tacked, right sides sewn
together, turned right side out, no batt

Fan Lover

QUILT SIZE: 48" x 48"
BLOCK SIZE: 12"
FABRICS
Centers: $1/8$ yard of 9 different fabrics
Strips: $1/4$ yard of 20 different fabrics
Foundation: $2^3/4$ yards
Backing: 2 yards

Mona has been quilting since 1992 and enjoys the added challenge of using a variety of fabrics for each quilt. This quilt has a multitude of colors using an original fan design adapted from the fan in *The New Sampler Quilt* by Diana Leone, 1980, and incorporating crazy patchwork. Mona purchased 100 fat quarters (18" x 22" pieces of fabric) just to get started.

Creating an original fan design and combining the methods used for a crazy quilt, provide a beauty of movement and richness. The multitude of fabrics really makes this quilt a unique collection of textures and colors. The fabrics were sewn to a 13" x 13" muslin foundation in crazy quilt style, and then the pieced fan was hand appliquéd to the block. The blocks were trimmed to $12^1/2$" and sewn together, using a $1/4$" seam allowance, to form the top. No batting was used; the muslin foundations of each block became the batting. The quilt was assembled using the easy no-binding technique (without batting) on page 25, steps 4–9.

See page 92 for fan template.

12" block, appliquéd, pieced fan, crazy pieced background on foundation fabric

CAT CRAZY, 1995
Kei N. Palmer
machine pieced, hand quilted, embellished with crazy
quilt stitches

Cat Crazy

QUILT SIZE: 43" x 43"

BLOCK SIZE: 12"

FABRICS

Centers: 6" x 6" pieces or $1/4$ yard each of 9 different fabrics

Strips: $1/8$ yards each of 43 different fabrics

Foundation: $1^1/4$ yards of lightweight cotton

Border: $3/4$ yard

Backing: $1^3/4$ yards of one fabric or leftovers from the front fabrics

Batting: 49" x 49"

Binding: $3/4$ yard

Kei wanted to use every cat and kitten print from her collection in one quilt. She found the cotton crazy quilt the answer. The top was machine pieced. Crazy quilt stitches were added to the top by hand.

12" block with 5-sided center

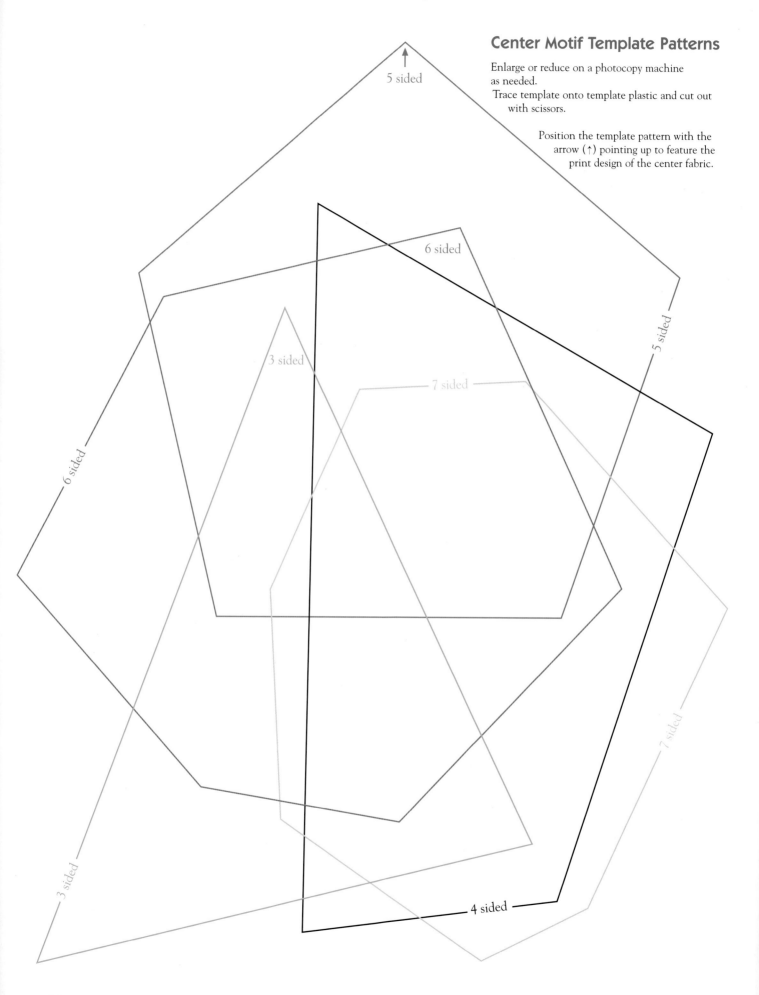

Center Motif Template Patterns

Enlarge or reduce on a photocopy machine as needed.
Trace template onto template plastic and cut out with scissors.

Position the template pattern with the arrow (↑) pointing up to feature the print design of the center fabric.

5 sided

6 sided

3 sided

7 sided

5 sided

6 sided

7 sided

3 sided

4 sided

Fan Patterns

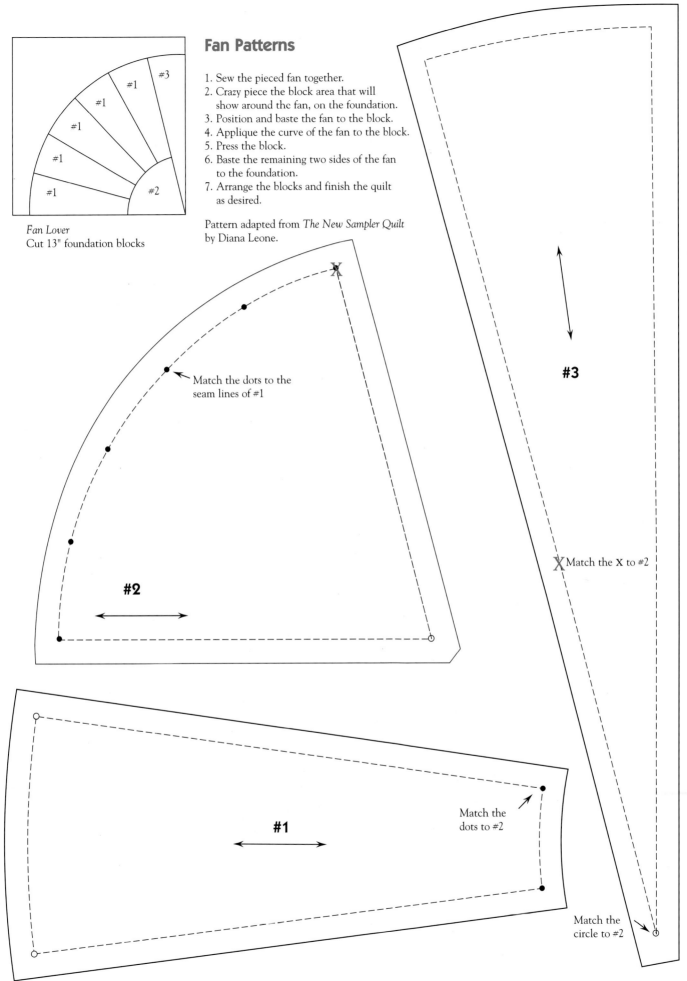

1. Sew the pieced fan together.
2. Crazy piece the block area that will show around the fan, on the foundation.
3. Position and baste the fan to the block.
4. Applique the curve of the fan to the block.
5. Press the block.
6. Baste the remaining two sides of the fan to the foundation.
7. Arrange the blocks and finish the quilt as desired.

Pattern adapted from *The New Sampler Quilt* by Diana Leone.

Fan Lover
Cut 13" foundation blocks

#1 #1 #1 #1 #1 #1 #2 #3

Match the dots to the seam lines of #1

#2

#3

X Match the **X** to #2

#1

Match the dots to #2

Match the circle to #2

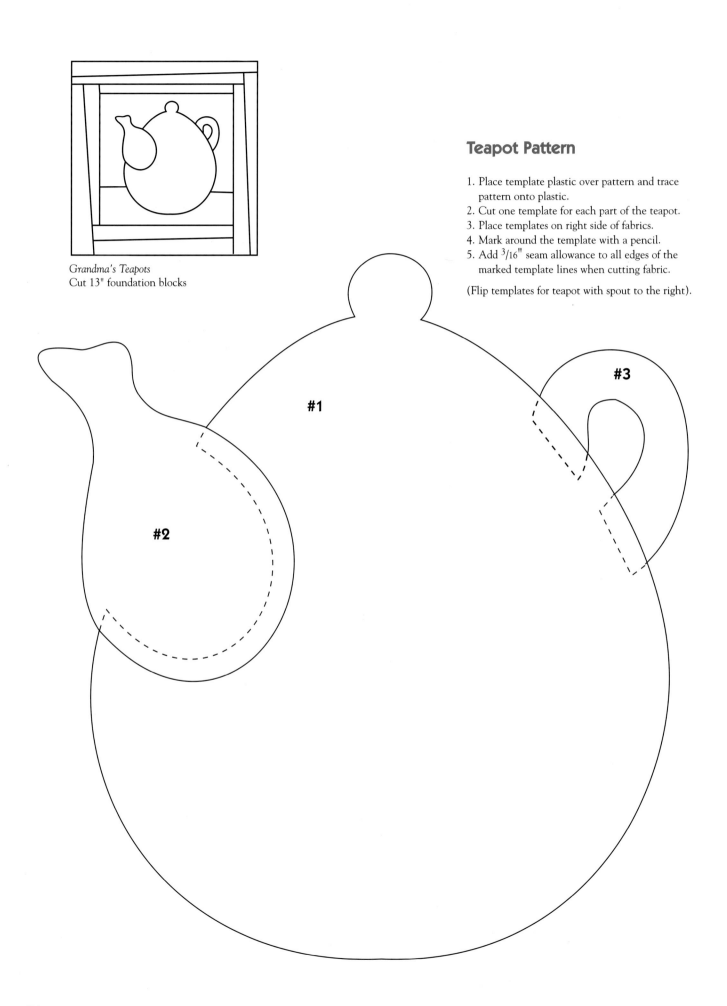

Grandma's Teapots
Cut 13" foundation blocks

Teapot Pattern

1. Place template plastic over pattern and trace pattern onto plastic.
2. Cut one template for each part of the teapot.
3. Place templates on right side of fabrics.
4. Mark around the template with a pencil.
5. Add $^3/_{16}$" seam allowance to all edges of the marked template lines when cutting fabric.

(Flip templates for teapot with spout to the right).

#1

#2

#3

Bibliography

Bond, Dorothy. *Crazy Quilt Stitches*. Bond Publications: Cottage Grove, OR, 1981.

Bradkin, Cheryl Greider. *Basic Seminole Patchwork*. C&T Publishing: Lafayette, CA, 1990.

Hargrave, Harriet. *Heirloom Machine Quilting*. C&T Publishing: Lafayette, CA, 1995.

Leone, Diana. *Attic Windows—A Contemporary View*. Leone Publications: Mountain View, CA, 1988.

Leone, Diana. *Fine Hand Quilting*. Leone Publications: Mountain View, CA, 1986.

Leone, Diana. *The New Sampler Quilt Book*. C&T Publishing: Lafayette, CA, 1996.

Meller, Susan & Joost Elffers. *Textile Designs*. Harry N. Abrams, Inc: New York, 1991.

Montano, Judith. *The Art of Silk Ribbon Embroidery*. C&T Publishing: Lafayette, CA, 1993.

Montano, Judith. *The Crazy Quilt Handbook*. C&T Publishing: Lafayette, CA, 1986.

Montano, Judith. *Crazy Quilt Odyssey*. C&T Publishing: Lafayette, CA, 1986.

Simms, Ami. *Creating Scrapbook Quilts*. Mallery Press: Flint, MI, 1993.

Other Fine Books From C&T Publishing:

An Amish Adventure - 2nd Edition, Roberta Horton

Appliqué 12 Easy Ways! Elly Sienkiewicz

Art & Inspiration: Ruth B. McDowell, Ruth B. McDowell

The Art of Silk Ribbon Embroidery, Judith Baker Montano

The Artful Ribbon, Candace Kling

Basic Seminole Patchwork, Cheryl Greider Bradkin

Beyond the Horizon, Small Landscape Appliqué, Valerie Hearder

Buttonhole Stitch Appliqué, Jean Wells

Colors Changing Hue, Yvonne Porcella

Crazy Quilt Handbook, Judith Montano

Crazy Quilt Odyssey, Judith Montano

Elegant Stitches: An Illustrated Stitch Guide & Source Book of Inspiration, Judith Baker Montano

Everything Flowers, Quilts from the Garden, Jean and Valori Wells

The Fabric Makes the Quilt, Roberta Horton

Fractured Landscape Quilts, Katie Pasquini Masopust

Heirloom Machine Quilting, Harriet Hargrave

Kaleidoscopes & Quilts, Paula Nadelstern

Impressionist Quilts, Gai Perry

Landscapes & Illusions, Joen Wolfrom

The Magical Effects of Color, Joen Wolfrom

Mariner's Compass: An American Quilt Classic, Judy Mathieson

Mariner's Compass Quilts, New Directions, Judy Mathieson

Mastering Machine Appliqué, Harriet Hargrave

The New Sampler Quilt, Diana Leone

Patchwork Quilts Made Easy, (co-published with Rodale Press) Jean Wells

Pattern Play, Doreen Speckmann

Pieces of an American Quilt, Patty McCormick

Quilts for Fabric Lovers, Alex Anderson

Quilts, Quilts, and More Quilts! Diana McClun and Laura Nownes

Schoolhouse Appliqué: Reverse Techniques and More, Charlotte Patera

Simply Stars, Alex Anderson

Small Scale Quiltmaking: Precision, Proportion, and Detail, Sally Collins

Soft-Edge Piecing, Jinny Beyer

Stripes in Quilts, Mary Mashuta

Tradition with a Twist: Variations on Your Favorite Quilts, Blanche Young and Dalene Young Stone

Trapunto by Machine, Hari Walner

A Treasury of Quilt Labels, Susan McKelvey

Visions QuiltArt, Quilt San Diego

The Visual Dance: Creating Spectacular Quilts, Joen Wolfrom

For more information write for a free catalog from:
C&T Publishing
P.O. Box 1456
Lafayette, CA 94549
(1-800-284-1114)

Buyer's Guide:

Please ask your favorite quilt shop to order any items you see or send your request to:

The Quilting Bee
357 Castro Street
Mountain View, CA 94041
1-888-QUILTER; 415-969-1714
Web Page: http://www.quiltingbee.com

Complete resource. All supplies, fabrics, machine accessories, books mentioned in this book are available by mail order from the Quilting Bee. Send your request for any item. We ship worldwide. This shop owned by the author, Diana Leone, is located forty miles south of San Francisco, off Highway 101. Be sure to visit when you are in Northern California. The trip will be worth your while.

Send $6 and a self-addressed, stamped envelope to receive The Quilting Bee catalog and newsletter, and request swatches of "theme" or any fabrics you are looking for.

About the Author

Diana Leone attended San Jose State University receiving a bachelor's degree, a Life Teaching credential, and a Master's Degree in Art and Education.

Diana's first quilts were the "Earth" series made for her Master's Exhibit at San Jose State in 1973.

Diana taught art in the public school system for thirteen years while raising her two sons, Eddie, Jr. and Joe. In 1975 she opened the Quilting Bee in Los Altos, California. This shop has grown to be one of the largest most complete quilter resource centers and is currently located in Mt. View, California.

The author of seven books, Diana leads a full life, quilting, writing, designing fabric, painting, teaching, traveling; and most of all, enjoying her two grandchildren.

Threads of Life, 1994, Diana Leone
Collection of Mr. and Mrs. Rolf Gass, Arova Mettler AG, Switzerland